# CATERING for SPECIAL OCCASIONS
## with
# MENUS & RECIPES

by
Fannie Merritt Farmer
Author of
"The Boston Cooking School Cook Book"

Illustrated with Half Tone Engravings
of Set Tables

Decorations
by
Albert D. Blashfield

Creative Cookbooks
Monterey, California

# Catering for Special Occasions with Menus & Recipes

by
## Fannie Merritt Farmer

ISBN 1-58963-279-6

Illustrared with Half Tone Engravings of Set Tables
Decorations by Albert D. Blashfield

Copyright © 2001 by Fredonia Books

Reprinted from the 1911 edition

Creative Cookbooks
An imprint of Fredonia Books
Monterey, California
http://www.creativecookbooks.com

All rights reserved, including the right to reproduce this book, or portions thereof, in any form.

In order to make original editions of historical works available to scholars at an economical price, this facsimile of the original edition of 1911 is reproduced from the best available copy and has been digitally enhanced to improve legibility, but the text remains unaltered to retain historical authenticity.

Catering for Special Occasions
*with*
MENUS AND RECIPES

"You must come home with me and be
  my guest;
You will give joy to me, and I will do
All that is in my power to honour you."

*Shelley*

AN AFTERNOON TEA TABLE.

# A FOREWORD

AMERICANS of to-day are accused, somewhat unjustly, it seems to me, of being inhospitable. Because we do not, in the manner of a generation or two ago, lay aside all our duties at the visit of friends and welcome them ungrudgingly to our ordinary meal we expose ourselves to this charge; but, in truth, it is a higher conception of hospitality that has brought about this change. In these days of rapid transit, by sea as well as by land, the markets of the world are brought almost to our very doors, and we have a hundred combinations to our grandmother's one. We, therefore, receive our guests more formally; we make preparations for their coming, and take pleasure in giving them a meal which shall vary from the humdrum order of culinary production. The fashion in entertaining, as in so many other things, has changed, and consciously or unconsciously we conform to the new standards. And why, on the whole, is

not the new hospitality more satisfying, both to the host and guest, than the old? It seems to me that housekeepers are enjoying as never before the days set apart for their friends, and have learned to appreciate the saying of Brillat-Savarin, "He who receives friends, without himself bestowing some pains upon the repast prepared for them, does not deserve to have friends." And certainly there is none of us so regardless of the delights of the table that he does not respond to the warming influences of a meal prepared by a thoughtful hostess as a tribute to him as a guest.

The difficulty for the housekeeper lies in the selection of an appropriate menu. This little book is intended to meet this difficulty. May it be a help to many!

Let me ask you to remember that all the recipes have been thoroughly tested, and not found wanting. You should have in mind, too, that in all these rules of mine the measurements are made level. Measuring cups, divided into thirds and quarters, are used, also tea and tablespoons.

With these words let me leave you to the enjoyment of the new hospitality!

FANNIE MERRITT FARMER.

# CONTENTS

|  | PAGE |
|---|---|
| NEW YEAR'S AFTERNOON TEAS | 1 |
| ST. VALENTINE'S SPREADS | 27 |
| WASHINGTON'S BIRTHDAY SPREADS | 51 |
| ST. PATRICK'S DAY LUNCHEONS | 69 |
| EASTER DINNERS | 87 |
| FOURTH OF JULY SPREADS | 105 |
| HALLOWE'EN SPREADS | 127 |
| THANKSGIVING DINNERS | 143 |
| CHRISTMAS DINNERS | 165 |
| WEDDING RECEPTIONS | 185 |
| BIRTHDAY FEASTING | 201 |
| CHILDREN'S PARTIES | 219 |

# ILLUSTRATIONS

| | PAGE |
|---|---|
| AN AFTERNOON TEA TABLE . . *Frontispiece*. | |
| TABLE LAID FOR ST. VALENTINE'S SPREAD . | 26 |
| A ST. PATRICK'S DAY LUNCHEON . . . . . | 68 |
| AN EASTER DINNER TABLE . . . . . . . | 86 |
| FOURTH OF JULY RECEPTION TABLE . . . | 105 |
| A THANKSGIVING DINNER TABLE . . . | 142 |
| A CHRISTMAS DINNER TABLE . . . . . . . | 165 |

# NEW YEAR'S AFTERNOON TEAS

MENU NO. I.

*"A cup and a welcome for everyone."*

Attleboro Sandwiches        Jam Jumbles

Salted Almonds         Five O'clock Tea

4   New Year's Afternoon Teas

### ATTLEBORO SANDWICHES

Spread thin unsweetened wafer crackers with peach conserve. Cover with wafers and arrange on a fancy plate covered with a doiley.

### PEACH CONSERVE

1 lb. dried peaches   Juice 1 orange
4 cups cold water    1 orange, thinly sliced
Juice 1 lemon        1 lb. sugar
1 cup raisins, seeded and cut in pieces
½ lb. English walnut meats cut in pieces

Soak peaches in water over night, add remaining ingredients, bring to the boiling-point, and let simmer one and one-fourth hours.

### JAM JUMBLES

½ cup butter       ½ cup sour milk
1 cup sugar        ¼ teaspoon salt
1 egg              Flour
½ teaspoon soda    Raspberry jam

Cream the butter, add sugar gradually, egg well beaten, soda mixed with milk, salt and flour to make a soft dough. Chill, roll to one-fourth inch in thickness, and shape, using a round cutter. On the centres of one-half the pieces put raspberry jam. Make three small openings

## New Year's Afternoon Teas

in remaining halves (forming a triangle), using a thimble, and put pieces together. Press edges slightly, and bake in a rather hot oven, that jumbles may keep good shape.

### WALNUT MERINGUE SQUARES

1½ cups of sugar    2 tablespoons shredded cocoanut
½ cup water         ¼ teaspoon vanilla
5 marshmallows      1 cup English walnut meats
Whites 2 eggs       2½ inch pastry squares

Cook sugar and water in smooth graniteware saucepan until syrup will spin a thread when dropped from tip of spoon. Remove to back of range and add marshmallows cut in small pieces. Pour gradually, while beating constantly, on to the whites of eggs beaten until stiff, then add cocoanut, vanilla, and chopped nut meats. Roll paste to one-eighth inch in thickness, cut in two and one-half inch squares, arrange on tin and spread with mixture, piling slightly. Bake in a moderate oven.

### SALTED ALMONDS

Blanch one-fourth pound Jordan almonds and dry on a towel. Put one-third cup olive oil in a very small saucepan. When hot, put in one-

6     New Year's Afternoon Teas

fourth of the almonds and fry until delicately browned, stirring to keep almonds constantly in motion. Remove with a spoon or small skimmer, taking up as little oil as possible. Drain on brown paper and sprinkle with salt, repeat until all are fried. It may be necessary to remove some of the salt by wiping nuts with a napkin.

To blanch almonds, cover with boiling water and let stand two minutes; drain, put into cold water, and rub off the skins.

### FIVE O'CLOCK TEA

Put three teaspoons tea in teapot and pour on two cups boiling water. Let stand three minutes and strain into tea cups. Serve with cut sugar and cream.

## MENU NO. II.

*"And while the bubbling and loud hissing urn*
*Throws up a steamy column, and the cups,*
*That cheer but not inebriate, wait on each,*
*So let us welcome peaceful evening in,"*
                                    Cowper.

Devonshire Sandwiches    Buttered Educators

'Scotch Five O'Clock Teas    Sultana Sticks

Hickory Nougat    Russian Tea

Hot Chocolate with Whipped Cream

# 8 New Year's Afternoon Teas

### DEVONSHIRE SANDWICHES

Cut Graham or entire wheat bread in one-fourth inch slices. Spread sparingly with butter and then with orange marmalade. Put together in pairs, remove crusts and cut in fancy shapes. Arrange on a plate covered with a doiley.

To offer variety the marmalade may sometimes be sprinkled with chopped pecan nut meats.

### ORANGE MARMALADE

9 oranges     8 lbs sugar
4 lemons     4 quarts water

Wipe fruit and cut crosswise in as thin slices as possible, removing seeds. Put into preserving kettle, add water, cover, and let stand thirty-six hours. Place on range, bring to boiling-point, and let simmer two hours. Add sugar and let simmer one hour. Turn into sterilized jelly tumblers and cover each glass with a circular piece of paraffine paper, then with a large circular piece of letter paper, fastening paper securely over edge of glass with mucilage.

### BUTTERED EDUCATORS

Spread Educator crackers sparingly with soft butter. Put in a dripping pan and bake in a

moderate oven until thoroughly heated. Cool and pile on a plate covered with a lace paper doiley.

### SCOTCH FIVE O'CLOCK TEAS

¾ lb. butter      6 ozs. sugar
1 lb. flour

Work the butter, using a wooden spoon, until very creamy; then add, gradually, while beating constantly, sugar. Work in the flour a little at a time, using the hands. Press evenly into a buttered dripping pan and prick with a fork. Bake in a moderate oven thirty minutes, and cut into small squares or strips. Let stand ten minutes before removing from pan. Pile on a plate covered with a doiley.

### SULTANA STICKS

1 cup sugar      ¾ teaspoon vanilla
¼ cup melted butter      ½ cup flour
1 egg, unbeaten      ¼ cup English walnut meats,
2 squares Baker's chocolate,    cut in pieces
    melted      ¼ cup Sultana raisins, cut in pieces

Mix ingredients in order given. Line a seven-inch square pan with paraffine paper. Spread

mixture evenly in pan, using a case knife, and bake in a slow oven. As soon as taken from oven, turn from pan, remove paper, and cut cake in strips three and one-half inches by one inch, using a sharp knife. If these directions are not followed, paper will cling to cake and it will be impossible to cut it in shapely pieces.

### HICKORY NOUGAT

2¼ cups sugar     ¼ teaspoon salt
1 cup chopped hickory nut meats

Put sugar in a perfectly smooth granite saucepan, place on range, and stir constantly until melted to a syrup, taking care to keep sugar from sides of pan. Add nut meats, pour at once into two warm buttered tins, seven inches by seven inches, and mark in small squares. If sugar is not removed from range as soon as melted, it will quickly caramelize.

### RUSSIAN TEA

Make same as Five O'Clock Tea, and allow one-half teaspoon lemon juice and a thin slice of lemon from which seeds have been removed to each cup. Sweeten with cut sugar to suit individual taste. Many prefer the addition of three whole cloves or a candied cherry.

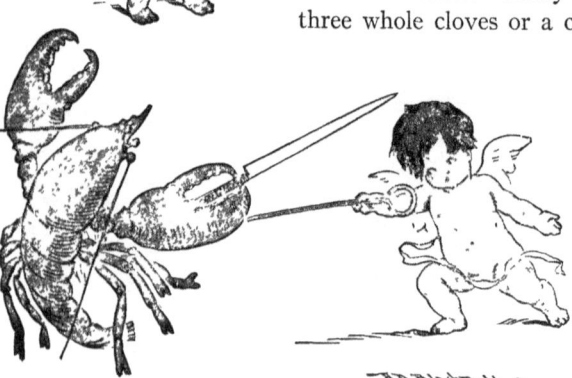

## HOT CHOCOLATE

1½ squares Baker's unsweet-   Few grains salt
ened chocolate   1 cup boiling water
¼ cup sugar   3 cups milk

Scald milk. Melt chocolate in small saucepan placed over hot water, add sugar, salt, and, gradually, boiling water; when smooth, place on range and boil one minute, add to scalded milk, mill, and serve in chocolate cups with whipped cream.

To mill chocolate, beat, using a Dover egg-beater until froth forms on top, preventing scum, which is so unsightly.

## WHIPPED CREAM

¾ cup thick cream   ⅓ cup powdered sugar
¼ cup milk   ½ teaspoon vanilla
White 1 egg

Mix cream and milk, beat until stiff, using egg-beater; add sugar, vanilla, and white of egg beaten until stiff.

MENU NO. III.

*"Tea! thou soft, thou sober sage; and venerable liquid;
Thou female tongue-running, smile-smoothing, heart-opening, wink-tippling cordial."*

Noisette Sandwiches        Peanut Crisps

Rochester Sandwiches     Florida Orange Sticks

Turkish Delight

Iced Tea             Five O'Clock Cocoa

## NOISETTE SANDWICHES

Cut Quick Nut Loaf in thin slices and spread with butter worked until creamy. Put together in pairs, remove crusts, cut in fancy shapes, and arrange on a plate covered with a lace paper doiley.

## QUICK NUT LOAF

| | |
|---|---|
| 2 cups bread flour | 2 tablespoons lard |
| ⅓ cup sugar | 1 egg |
| 4 teaspoons baking powder | 1 egg yolk |
| 1 teaspoon salt | 1 cup milk |
| 3 tablespoons butter | ½ cup English walnut meats |

Mix and sift flour, sugar, baking powder, and salt. Work in butter and lard, using tips of fingers; then add whole egg and egg yolk, well beaten; milk and nut meats, cut in pieces. Beat well, turn into a buttered bread pan, let stand twenty-five minutes, and bake in a moderate oven. Let stand twenty-four hours before using.

## PEANUT CRISPS

Spread thinly and evenly wheat crispies, or any small unsweetened wafer cracker, with peanut butter. Put in a dripping pan and bake in a hot oven until delicately browned. Arrange on a fancy plate covered with a doiley.

## ROCHESTER SANDWICHES

¼ cup butter         1 oz Baker's chocolate
½ cup sugar         2 tablespoons milk
1 egg                    1¼ cups flour
Few grains salt    1 teaspoon baking powder

Cream butter and add gradually, while beating constantly, sugar, then add egg well beaten, salt, and melted chocolate. Beat thoroughly and add milk alternately with flour, mixed and sifted with baking powder. Chill, roll very thin, shape with a small cutter, first dipped in flour, and bake on a buttered sheet. Cool and put together in pairs with the following mixture:

Work a cream cheese until smooth and moisten with cream until of right consistency to spread. Season highly with salt and paprika.

## FLORIDA ORANGE STICKS

½ cup butter              Grated rind 1 orange
1½ cups sugar            1½ cups flour
Yolks 4 eggs              ½ cup cornstarch
½ cup orange juice    4 teaspoons baking powder
                 Whites 4 eggs

Cream the butter and add gradually, while beating constantly, sugar; then add the yolks of eggs beaten until thick, orange juice, and grated rind. Mix flour, cornstarch, and baking powder. Combine mixtures and add whites of eggs beaten

until stiff. Bake in a buttered dripping pan, sprinkled generously with chopped walnut meats and sparingly with powdered sugar. Bake in a moderate oven twenty-five minutes. Remove from pan, cut in halves crosswise, and put together with orange filling; then cut in finger-shaped pieces and arrange on a plate, covered with a doiley.

### ORANGE FILLING

| | |
|---|---|
| 1 tablespoon butter | ⅓ cup sugar |
| 3 tablespoons powdered sugar | Yolk 1 egg |
| 2 tablespoons flour | ¼ cup orange juice |
| Grated rind ¼ orange | 1 teaspoon lemon juice |

Work butter until creamy and add gradually, while beating constantly, powdered sugar. Mix flour, sugar, and egg yolk slightly beaten. Add orange juice and cook, stirring constantly until mixture thickens.

### TURKISH DELIGHT

| | |
|---|---|
| 1 oz. red sheet gelatine | Juice 1 orange |
| ½ cup cold water | Juice 1 lemon |
| 1 lb. sugar | Grated rind 1 orange |
| ½ cup hot water | 1 tablespoon rum |
| ½ cup chopped nut meats | |

Soak gelatine broken in pieces in cold water two hours. Bring sugar and hot water to the

## New Year's Afternoon Teas

boiling-point, add soaked gelatine, and let simmer twenty minutes. Add remaining ingredients and turn into a pan (first dipped in cold water) to one inch in thickness.

Let stand until cold, remove from pan to board dredged with confectioners' sugar, cut in cubes, and roll in sugar.

The rum and nuts may be omitted.

### ICED TEA

Make same as Five O'Clock Tea, using four teaspoons tea, and strain at once over cracked ice. Serve in glasses one-fourth full of cracked ice. Sweeten to taste and allow two thin slices of lemon from which seeds have been removed or three crushed fresh mint leaves to each glass.

### FIVE O'CLOCK COCOA

3 tablespoons cocoa  
¼ cup sugar  
¾ cup boiling water  
A few grains salt  
4 cups milk  
2 teaspoons brandy  
½ teaspoon vanilla

Scald milk. Mix cocoa, sugar, and salt, adding enough boiling water to make a smooth paste; add remaining water and boil one minute; pour into scalded milk and add brandy and vanilla. Beat two minutes, using Dover egg-beater. Serve in chocolate cups with whipped cream.

# New Year's Afternoon Teas

## MENU NO. IV.

*" I, too, remember well that cheerful bowl
Which round his table flow'd.  The serious there
Mix'd with the sportive, with the learn'd the plain;
Mirth soften'd wisdom, candour temper'd mirth'
And wit its honey lent, without the sting."*
                                            Thompson.

Lobster Patties            Huntington Chicken

Tea Rolls            Orange Honey Sandwiches

Pineapple Mousse                   Macaroons

Silver Sponge Cakes           Oriental Punch

20   New Year's Afternoon Teas

## LOBSTER PATTIES

Fill patty shells with lobster filling, arrange on a serving dish, and garnish with parsley.

## PATTY SHELLS

Roll puff paste one-quarter inch thick, shape with a patty cutter, first dipped in flour; remove centres from one-half the rounds with smaller cutter. Brush over with cold water the larger pieces near the edge, and fit on rings, pressing lightly. Place in towel between pans of crushed ice, and chill until paste is stiff; if cold weather, chill out of doors. Place on iron or tin sheet covered with brown paper, and bake twenty-five minutes in hot oven. The shells should rise their full height and begin to brown in twelve to fifteen minutes; continue browning, and finish baking in twenty-five minutes Pieces cut from centre of rings of patties may be baked and used for patty covers, or put together, rolled, and cut for unders.

## LOBSTER FILLING

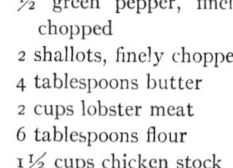

½ green pepper, finely chopped
2 shallots, finely chopped
4 tablespoons butter
2 cups lobster meat
6 tablespoons flour
1½ cups chicken stock

2 tablespoons sherry
2 tablespoons sauterne
½ teaspoon paprika
¾ teaspoon salt
Few grains pepper
⅓ cup cream
Yolks 2 eggs

# New Year's Afternoon Teas

Cook pepper and shallot with butter until butter is slightly browned, then add lobster meat and cook five minutes. Add flour and stir until well blended, then pour on gradually while stirring constantly chicken stock. Bring to the boiling-point, add seasonings, and just before serving, cream and yolks of eggs.

## HUNTINGTON CHICKEN

1 tablespoon granulated gelatine
¾ cup hot chicken stock
¾ cup heavy cream
1½ cups cold cooked chicken, cut in dice
½ tablespoon granulated gelatine
2 tablespoons cold water
Yolks 2 eggs
1 teaspoon salt
1½ teaspoons sugar
1 teaspoon mustard
¼ teaspoon pepper
2 tablespoons lemon juice
1 tablespoon vinegar
½ cup hot cream
1½ tablespoons butter
Whites 2 eggs
½ cup heavy cream
2 cups finely chopped celery

Dissolve one tablespoon gelatine in chicken stock and strain. When mixture begins to thicken, beat until frothy, and add three-fourths cup heavy cream, beaten until stiff, and chicken dice. Season with salt and pepper, turn into individual molds, and chill. Soak remaining gelatine in cold water, dissolve by standing over hot water, then strain. Beat yolks of eggs

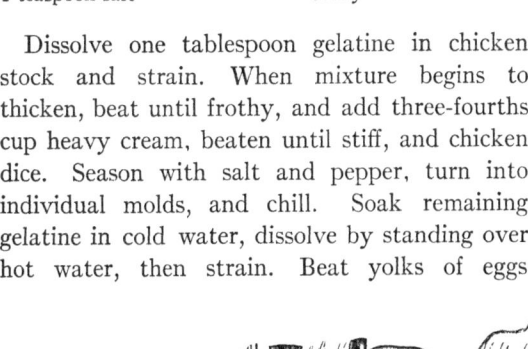

slightly and add salt, sugar, mustard, lemon juice, vinegar, and hot cream. Cook over hot water until mixture thickens, add butter and strained gelatine. Add mixture gradually to whites of eggs beaten stiff, and when cold, fold in heavy cream beaten until stiff, and celery. Remove chicken from mold, surround with sauce, and garnish with celery tips.

## TEA ROLLS

| 1 cup scalded milk | 2 tablespoons lard |
| 1½ tablespoons sugar | 1 yeast cake |
| 1 teaspoon salt | ¼ cup lukewarm water |
| 2 tablespoons butter | White 1 egg |
| 3½ cups flour | |

Add sugar, salt, butter, and lard to scalded milk, and when lukewarm add yeast cake, dissolved in lukewarm water, white of one egg well beaten, and flour. Cover, let rise, toss on a floured board, roll in a long strip one-fourth inch in thickness, spread with melted butter, roll up like a jelly roll, and cut in one-inch pieces. Place pieces in pan close together, flat side down, cover, let rise, and bake in a hot oven.

## ORANGE HONEY SANDWICHES

Cut white bread in thin slices, spread sparingly with creamed butter and orange honey. Put

together in pairs, remove crusts, and cut in finger-shaped pieces. Pile log-cabin fashion on a plate covered with a doiley.

### ORANGE HONEY

1 cup sugar
¼ cup water
½ teaspoon vanilla
¼ cup orange juice
½ cup orange peel, finely chopped

Bring sugar, water, and orange juice to the boiling-point and let boil until syrup will thread when dropped from tip of spoon. Add orange peel and vanilla, again bring to the boiling-point, and cool.

### PINEAPPLE MOUSSE

1 tablespoon granulated gelatine
¼ cup cold water
2 tablespoons lemon juice
1 cup sugar
1 quart cream
1 cup pineapple syrup

Heat one can shredded pineapple to the boiling-point and drain. To one cup of the syrup add gelatine soaked in cold water, lemon juice, and sugar. Strain and cool. As mixture thickens, fold in the whip from cream. Mold, pack in salt and ice, using equal parts, and let stand four hours.

## SILVER SPONGE CAKES

Whites 5 eggs   ½ teaspoon cream of tartar
¾ cup sugar   ½ cup bread flour
1 teaspoon vanilla

Beat whites of eggs until stiff and dry and add gradually, while beating constantly, sugar mixed and sifted with baking powder. Sift flour into the mixture, add flavoring, and cut and fold until well blended. Fill buttered gem pans two-thirds full, sprinkle with powdered sugar, and bake in a moderate oven.

## MACAROONS

½ lb. almond paste   Whites 3 eggs
⅜ lb. powdered sugar

Work together almond paste and sugar on a smooth board or marble slab. Then add whites of eggs gradually, and work until mixture is perfectly smooth. Confectioners at first use the hand, afterward a palette knife, which is not only of use for mixing but for keeping board clean. Shape, using a pastry bag and tube, on a tin sheet covered with buttered paper, one-half inch apart; or drop mixture from tip of spoon in small piles. Macaroon mixture is stiff enough to hold its shape, but in baking spreads. Bake fifteen to

twenty minutes in a slow oven. If liked soft, they should be slightly baked. After removing from oven, invert paper, and wet with a cloth wrung out of cold water, when macaroons will easily slip off. Almond paste may be bought in one-pound tins of any first class city grocer.

### ORIENTAL PUNCH

| | |
|---|---|
| 1 cup sugar | Juice 2 lemons |
| 1 cup water | Juice 3 oranges |
| 6 cloves | 1 drop oil of peppermint |
| 1 inch stick cinnamon | Green coloring |
| Preserved ginger | Fresh mint leaves |
| | Cake of ice |

Make a syrup by boiling sugar, water, cloves, stick cinnamon, and preserved ginger, the size of an English walnut, five minutes. Cool, add fruit juices, strain, add oil of peppermint and coloring. Cover and let stand one hour. Pour over a large cake of ice in punch bowl and garnish with mint leaves.

TABLE LAID FOR ST. VALENTINE'S SPREAD.

## ST. VALENTINE'S SPREADS

## MENU NO. I.

*"O, lady, there be many things
That seem right fair, below, above,
But sure, not one among them all
Is half so sweet as love."*
   Oliver Wendell Holmes.

Sweetbreads à la York

Ham Mousse    Honor Sandwiches

Coffee Caramel Parfait

Orange Hearts    Lord Baltimore Cake

Mint Tulip

## SWEETBREADS À LA YORK

Cover one pair sweetbreads with cold water and let stand thirty minutes. Drain, and cover with boiling water to which has been added one-half teaspoon salt, one-half tablespoon vinegar, one slice onion, one slice carrot, one sprig parsley, and one stalk celery cut in small pieces. Bring to the boiling-point and let simmer twenty minutes. Drain, plunge into cold water, again drain, add one-half cup sherry wine, cover, and let stand one hour. Peel one-fourth pound mushroom caps, cut in slices, and sauté in butter. Melt three tablespoons butter, add three tablespoons flour, and stir until well blended; then pour on gradually, while stirring constantly, one cup thin cream and one-half cup heavy cream. Bring to the boiling-point, add sweetbreads, drained from sherry and cut in small cubes, and mushrooms. Season with one teaspoon salt and one-fourth teaspoon paprika. Serve in heart-shaped timbale cases.

## TIMBALE CASES

¾ cup flour  
½ teaspoon salt  
1 teaspoon sugar  
½ cup milk  
1 egg  
1 tablespoon olive oil

## St. Valentine's Spreads

Mix dry ingredients, add milk gradually, and beaten egg; then add olive oil. Shape, using a hot, heart-shaped timbale iron, fry in deep fat until crisp and brown, take from iron and invert on brown paper to drain.

*To Heat Timbale Iron.*—Heat fat until nearly hot enough to fry uncooked mixtures. Put iron into hot fat, having fat deep enough to more than cover it, and let stand until heated. The only way of knowing when iron is of right temperature is to take it from fat, shake what fat may drip from it, lower in batter to three-fourths its depth, raise from batter, then immerse in hot fat. If batter does not cling to iron, or drops from iron as soon as immersed in fat, it is either too hot or not sufficiently heated.

*To Form Timbales.*—Turn timbale batter into a cup. Lower hot iron into cup, taking care that batter covers iron to only three-fourths its depth. When immersed in fat, mixture will rise to top of iron, and when crisp and brown may be easily slipped off. If too much batter is used, in cooking it will rise over top of iron, and in order to remove timbale it must be cut around with a sharp knife close to top of iron. If the cases are soft rather than crisp, batter is too thick and must be diluted with milk.

## HAM MOUSSE

2 cups finely chopped cooked ham  
1 teaspoon made mustard  
Few grains cayenne  
1 tablespoon granulated gelatine  
¼ cup cold water  
¼ cup hot water  
½ cup heavy cream

Pound chopped ham in a mortar with mustard and cayenne. Soak gelatine in cold water, dissolve in hot water and add to mixture, with cream beaten until stiff. Turn into mold. Chill, remove from mold to cold serving dish and garnish with parsley. Serve with

## EPICUREAN SAUCE

1 tablespoon tarragon vinegar  
2 tablespoons grated horse-radish root  
1 teaspoon English mustard  
½ teaspoon salt  
Few grains cayenne  
½ cup heavy cream  
3 tablespoons Mayonnaise dressing

Mix first five ingredients, then add cream beaten until stiff and Mayonnaise dressing.

## HONOR SANDWICHES

Cut white bread in one-fourth inch slices, and shape with heart cutter. Spread with pimiento butter, put together in pairs, and arrange on a fancy plate covered with a doiley.

## St. Valentine's Spreads

### PIMIENTO BUTTER

Cream two tablespoons butter, add one canned pimiento forced through a sieve, and work until thoroughly blended; then season with salt.

### COFFEE CARAMEL PARFAIT

| 1 cup milk | Yolks 3 eggs |
|---|---|
| 2 tablespoons ground coffee | ⅛ teaspoon salt |
| 1 cup sugar | 3 cups cream |
| 1 teaspoon vanilla | |

Scald milk with coffee and add one-half the sugar that has been caramelized, then add yolks of eggs mixed with remaining sugar and salt. Cook until mixture thickens, stirring constantly, and add one cup thin cream. Cool, strain, add two cups thin cream, and vanilla. Freeze, using three parts finely crushed ice to one part rock salt. Pack in one-half pound baking powder boxes, filling boxes to overflowing. Adjust covers, pack in salt and ice, using equal parts, and let stand two hours. Remove from molds to cold platter and roll in Jordan almonds blanched, cut in thin slices, and delicately browned in a moderate oven.

### ORANGE HEARTS

Roll paste to one-fourth inch in thickness, and shape with a small heart-shaped cutter,

first dipped in flour. Arrange on an unbuttered tin sheet and bake until delicately browned. Split, fill with orange marmalade, frost with orange frosting, and sprinkle chopped candied orange peel around edge.

### ORANGE FROSTING

Grated rind 1 orange  
1 teaspoon brandy  
½ teaspoon lemon juice  
1 tablespoon orange juice  
Yolk 1 egg  
Confectioners' sugar

Add rind to brandy and fruit juices. Cover and let stand fifteen minutes. Strain and add gradually, while stirring constantly, to egg yolk slightly beaten. Stir in confectioners' sugar until of right consistency to spread.

### ORANGE MARMALADE

9 oranges  
4 lemons  
8 lbs sugar  
4 qts. cold water

Wipe fruit and cut crosswise in as thin slices as possible, removing seeds. Put into a preserving kettle, cover with water, and let stand thirty-six hours. Place on range, bring to the boiling-point, and let simmer two hours Add sugar and let simmer one hour. Turn into sterilized jelly tumblers and cover each glass with a circular

## St. Valentine's Spreads

piece of paraffine paper, then with a larger circular piece of letter paper, fastening paper securely over edge of glass with mucilage.

### LORD BALTIMORE CAKE

½ cup butter   ½ cup milk
1 cup sugar   1¾ cups flour
Yolks 8 eggs   4 teaspoons baking powder
2 teaspoons vanilla

Cream butter and add sugar gradually while beating constantly, then add yolks of eggs, beaten until thick and lemon-colored, milk, flour, mixed and sifted with baking powder, and vanilla. Bake in three buttered and floured seven-inch square tins. Put layers together with Lord Baltimore Filling and cover top and sides with Ice Cream Frosting.

### LORD BALTIMORE FILLING

Beat ice cream frosting without flavoring until cold and add one-half cup rolled dry macaroons, one-fourth cup each chopped almonds and pecans, twelve candied cherries cut in quarters, two teaspoons lemon juice, three teaspoons sherry wine, and one-fourth teaspoon orange extract.

### ICE CREAM FROSTING

1½ cups sugar   Whites 2 eggs
½ cup water   ½ teaspoon vanilla

Cook sugar and water in a smooth graniteware saucepan until syrup will spin a long thread when dropped from tip of spoon. Pour gradually, while beating constantly, on to the whites of eggs beaten until stiff (but not dry), add flavoring, and continue the beating until mixture is of the right consistency to spread.

### MINT TULIP

5 lemons  
1 bunch fresh mint  
1½ cups sugar  
½ cup water  
3 bottles ginger ale  
Ice

Squeeze the juice from lemons, add leaves from mint, sugar, and water. Let stand thirty minutes, add a large piece of ice and ginger ale. Serve in small glasses.

# St. Valentine's Spreads

## MENU NO. II.

*" The yearly course that brings this day about
Shall never see it but a holiday."*

Scalloped Scallops        Chicken Jelly Salad

Cadillac Cheese Sandwiches

Pineapple Sponge          Cinkites

Lady Fingers              Coffee

## St. Valentine's Spreads

### SCALLOPED SCALLOPS

| | |
|---|---|
| 1 pint scallops | Salt |
| ½ cup melted butter | Pepper |
| 1 cup cracker crumbs | ⅔ cup cream |
| ½ cup soft bread crumbs | |

Wash and pick over scallops. Mix cracker and bread crumbs and add butter. Cover the bottom of a buttered dish with crumbs, add one-half the scallops. Sprinkle with salt and pepper and pour over one-half the cream, repeat, cover with remaining crumbs, and bake in a hot oven twenty-five minutes.

### CHICKEN JELLY SALAD

Disjoint a six-pound fowl, put in a kettle, add two quarts boiling water, cover, and let simmer until meat is tender. Remove fowl, and add to stock two stalks celery, bit of bay leaf, one small sliced onion, and salt and pepper to taste. Simmer two hours, when stock should be reduced to three pints. Strain, cool, and clear, using the whites and shells of two eggs; then add four tablespoons granulated gelatine.

Put a layer in bottom of mold, set in pan of ice water and, when firm, garnish with yolks of hard-boiled eggs, sliced and cut in fancy shapes, whites of hard boiled eggs, cut in fancy shapes, and truffles, sliced and cut in fancy shapes.

## St. Valentine's Spreads

Add more stock and, when firm, a layer of chicken meat, then more stock. Spread with a layer of paté-de-fois-gras, and repeat until mold is full. When firm, remove from mold to serving dish, surround with Mayonnaise dressing, and garnish with curled celery.

The paté-de-fois-gras may be omitted.

### CADILLAC CHEESE SANDWICHES

Cream one-half cup butter, add one-fourth pound Roquefort cheese, and stir until mixture is smooth; then add one-half teaspoon paprika, one teaspoon finely cut chives, and salt to taste. Moisten with two tablespoons sherry wine, spread between thin slices of bread (preferably Graham or rye), and cut into heart-shaped pieces. Arrange on a plate covered with a doiley.

### PINEAPPLE SPONGE

| | |
|---|---|
| Yolks 3 eggs | ⅔ cup grated pineapple |
| Grated rind and juice 1 lemon | 1½ tablespoons granulated gelatine |
| ½ cup sugar | ⅓ cup cold water |
| Few grains salt | ½ cup heavy cream |
| | Whites 3 eggs |

Beat egg yolks slightly and add grated rind, fruit juice, sugar, and salt. Cook, stirring constantly until mixture thickens. Remove from

## 40　St. Valentine's Spreads

fire, add pineapple and gelatine soaked five minutes in water. When mixture begins to thicken, add cream beaten until stiff and egg whites beaten until stiff. Turn into a mold first dipped in cold water and chill.

### CINKITES

Whites 3 eggs　　　1½ teaspoons cinnamon
½ lb. powdered sugar　½ lb. unblanched almonds
Rind ½ lemon

Beat egg whites until stiff and add sugar, lemon rind, cinnamon, and almonds finely chopped. Toss on a board sprinkled with flour, then with powdered sugar, and knead. Pat and roll to one-fourth inch in thickness.

Shape with a heart or any small fancy cutter, place on a buttered sheet, and bake in a moderate oven.

Glaze with

### CONFECTIONERS' FROSTING

To two tablespoons hot water add confectioners' (not powdered) sugar until of the right consistency to spread. Flavor with one-half teaspoon vanilla. Apply with a butter-brush.

St. Valentine's Spreads

## LADY FINGERS

Whites 3 eggs  ⅓ cup flour
⅓ cup powdered sugar  ⅛ teaspoon salt
Yolks 2 eggs  ¼ teaspoon vanilla

Beat whites of eggs until stiff and dry, add sugar gradually, and continue beating. Then add yolks of eggs beaten until thick and lemon-colored, and flavoring. Cut and fold in flour mixed and sifted with salt. Shape four and one-half inches long and one inch wide on a tin sheet covered with unbuttered paper, using a pastry bag and tube. Sprinkle with powdered sugar and bake eight minutes in a moderate oven. Remove from paper with a knife.

## St. Valentine's Luncheon

### MENU NO. III.

"*'Tis well to be merry and wise,
'Tis well to be honest and true,
'Tis well to be off with the old love
Before you are on with the new.*"

Thorndike Canapes

Manhattan Clam Bouillon

Fillets of Halibut à la Hollenden

Luncheon Rolls

Knickerbocker Suprême of Chicken

Martinique Potatoes

Lakewood Salad   Toasted Butter Thins

Chocolate Ice Cream   Marshmallow Sauce

Harvard Wafers   Mint Hearts

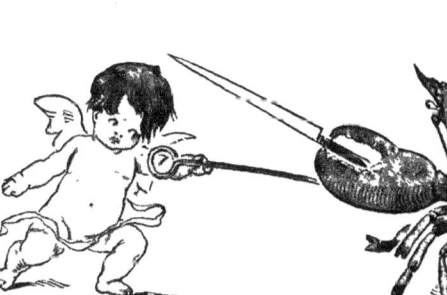

## THORNDIKE CANAPES

Cut stale bread in one-fourth inch slices and shape with a small heart cutter. Cream butter, add an equal quantity of grated Young America cheese, and work until smooth; then season with salt. Spread on bread and garnish with a one-fourth inch border of finely chopped olives and a piece of red or green pepper cut in heart shape, in center of each.

Serve each on a small plate covered with a lace paper doiley.

## MANHATTAN CLAM BOUILLON

| | |
|---|---|
| 2 qts. clams in shells | ½ teaspoon salt |
| Water | Paprika |
| 3 tablespoons butter | 1 cup cream |
| 3½ tablespoons flour | |

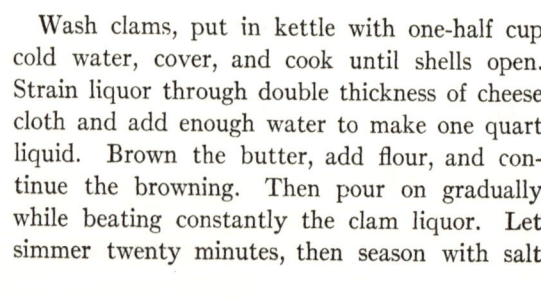

Wash clams, put in kettle with one-half cup cold water, cover, and cook until shells open. Strain liquor through double thickness of cheese cloth and add enough water to make one quart liquid. Brown the butter, add flour, and continue the browning. Then pour on gradually while beating constantly the clam liquor. Let simmer twenty minutes, then season with salt

# St. Valentine's Luncheon

and paprika. Just before serving add cream and serve in bouillon cups with

## PIMIENTO CREAM

Beat one-half cup heavy cream until stiff, using a Dover egg-beater. Add one-half the beaten white of an egg, two tablespoons pimiento purée, and a few grains salt. Pimiento purée is made from canned pimientos forced through a sieve.

## FILLETS OF HALIBUT À LA HOLLENDEN

| | |
|---|---|
| 2¾ lb. slices halibut | 3 tablespoons butter |
| 6 slices fat salt pork | 3 tablespoons flour |
| 1 onion | ¾ cup buttered cracker crumbs |

Wipe fish and cut into eight fillets. Arrange pork in pan, cover with onion thinly sliced and bay leaf. Place fish on pork, spread with butter worked until creamy and mixed with flour; sprinkle with buttered crumbs, and bake in a hot oven. Remove to hot serving dish and pour around the following sauce:

To two and one-half tablespoons fat remaining in pan add two tablespoons flour and stir until well blended; then pour on gradually while stirring

constantly one cup cream. Bring to the boiling-point and add one-fourth teaspoon salt, one-eighth teaspoon pepper, and one tablespoon butter, bit by bit.

### LUNCHEON ROLLS

½ cup scalded milk 2 tablespoons melted butter
2 tablespoons sugar 1 egg
¼ teaspoon salt Flour
½ yeast cake dissolved in 2 tablespoons lukewarm water

Add sugar and salt to milk; when lukewarm, add dissolved yeast cake and three-fourths cup flour. Cover and let rise; then add butter, egg well beaten, and enough flour to knead. Let rise again, roll to one-half inch thickness, shape with small round cutter first dipped in flour, place in buttered pan close together, let rise again, and bake. Brush over with two tablespoons milk mixed with one tablespoon sugar and return to oven to set glaze.

### KNICKERBOCKER SUPRÊME OF CHICKEN

Remove fillets (breast meat) from two young chickens and trim into shape. Sprinkle with salt and pepper, dip in cream, roll in flour and sauté in butter until delicately browned. Place in a

## St. Valentine's Luncheon

small pan, dot over with butter, and bake until tender. Remove to cutlet-shaped pieces of hot boiled ham (cut very thin), garnish top of each with three short stalks of asparagus, seasoned with butter, and pour around the following sauce:

Melt three and one-half tablespoons butter, add three and one-half tablespoons flour, and stir until well blended; then pour on gradually while stirring constantly one cup chicken stock and one-half cup cream. Bring to the boiling-point, season with salt and paprika, and add the yolk of one egg.

### MARTINIQUE POTATOES

Scoop out inside of four hot baked potatoes and force through a potato ricer. Add one and one-half tablespoons butter, the yolk of one egg, three tablespoons cream, one-half teaspoon salt, one-eighth teaspoon pepper, and a few grains nutmeg. Set on range and beat three minutes; then add gradually the white of one egg beaten to a stiff froth. Shape between two buttered tablespoons, place on a buttered sheet, and bake until delicately browned.

### LAKEWOOD SALAD

Remove pulp in sections from two grapefruits. Skin and seed three-fourths cup white grapes.

Cut one-third cup pecan nut meats in pieces. Arrange on a bed of romaine, pour over dressing, and garnish with strip of red pepper.

*For the Dressing.*—Mix four tablespoons olive oil, one tablespoon grapefruit juice, one-half tablespoon vinegar, one teaspoon salt, one-fourth teaspoon paprika, one-eighth teaspoon pepper, and one tablespoon finely chopped Roquefort cheese.

### CHOCOLATE ICE CREAM

| | |
|---|---|
| 2 cups scalded milk | 1 egg |
| 1 tablespoon flour | ⅛ teaspoon salt |
| 1¼ cups sugar | 3 squares Baker's chocolate |
| 1 qt thin cream | 2 tablespoons vanilla |

Mix flour, sugar, and salt, add egg slightly beaten, and milk gradually; cook over hot water twenty minutes, stirring constantly at first. Melt three squares chocolate by placing in a small saucepan set in a larger saucepan of boiling water, and pour hot custard slowly on chocolate. When cool, add cream and flavoring; strain and freeze. Serve in heart-shaped paper cases with Marshmallow Sauce on each.

### MARSHMALLOW SAUCE

¼ lb marshmallows      ¼ cup confectioners' sugar
¼ cup boiling water

## St. Valentine's Luncheon

Cut marshmallows in pieces and melt in double boiler. Dissolve sugar in boiling water, add to marshmallows, and stir until thoroughly blended. Cool before serving.

### HARVARD WAFERS

| | |
|---|---|
| ½ cup butter | 2 teaspoons baking powder |
| 1 cup sugar | White 1 egg |
| 1 egg | Chopped almonds |
| 2 cups flour | 1 tablespoon sugar |
| 2 tablespoons milk | ¼ teaspoon cinnamon |

Cream the butter, add sugar gradually, and egg well beaten and milk; then add flour mixed and sifted with baking powder. Chill, toss one-half mixture on a floured board, and roll one-eighth inch thick. Shape with heart cutter. Brush over with white of egg, and sprinkle with sugar mixed with cinnamon and almonds. Place on a buttered sheet and bake eight minutes in a slow oven.

# WASHINGTON'S BIRTHDAY SPREADS

# Washington's Birthday Spreads

## MENU NO. I.

*"Full character'd with lasting memory."*

Traymore Chicken Timbales

Salad Rolls

Chaufroid of Salmon

Fairmont Sandwiches

Almond Cream

Peanut Drops

George Washington Hatchets

Fruit Punch

## TRAYMORE CHICKEN TIMBALES

Force remnants of cold cooked chicken or boiled fowl through a meat chopper, then repeat; there should be one and one-half cups. Pound in a mortar and add gradually, while continuing the pounding, the yolks of three eggs and one-half cup heavy cream; then add one-third cup white wine. Fold in the whites of three eggs, beaten until stiff. Butter individual timbale molds and fill one-quarter full of white sauce, to which has been added one teaspoon finely chopped truffles or one-half tablespoon finely chopped green or red pepper.

Fill molds with chicken. Set in pans of hot water, cover with buttered paper, and bake until firm. Remove from mold to hot serving dish, when sauce will run down sides of timbales. Garnish with sprigs of parsley.

For the white sauce melt two tablespoons butter, add two tablespoons flour, and stir until well blended, then pour on gradually, while stirring constantly, one cup milk. Bring to the boiling-point and season with one-fourth teaspoon salt and a few grains pepper.

# Washington's Birthday Spreads

## SALAD ROLLS

| | |
|---|---|
| 1 cup scalded milk | 1 yeast cake dissolved in |
| ¼ cup shortening | ¼ cup lukewarm water |
| 1½ tablespoons sugar | White 1 egg |
| ½ teaspoon salt | 3¾ cups flour |

Add shortening, using half butter and half lard, sugar, and salt to milk; when lukewarm, add dissolved yeast cake, white of egg well beaten, and flour. Knead, let rise, toss on a floured board, and shape into small biscuits. Place in rows on a slightly floured board, cover with cloth and pan, and let rise until well puffed. Flour handle of wooden spoon and make a deep crease in middle of each biscuit, take up, and press. Place close together in buttered pan, cover, let rise, and bake fifteen minutes in hot oven.

## CHAUFROID OF SALMON

| | |
|---|---|
| 1 can salmon | Yolks 2 eggs |
| ½ tablespoon salt | 1½ tablespoons melted butter |
| 1½ tablespoons sugar | |
| ½ tablespoon flour | ¾ cup milk |
| 1 teaspoon mustard | ¼ cup vinegar |
| Few grains cayenne | ¾ tablespoon granulated gelatine |
| 2 tablespoons cold water | |

Remove salmon from can, rinse thoroughly with hot water, and separate in flakes. Mix dry ingredients, add egg yolks, butter, milk, and vinegar.

## 56   Washington's Birthday Spreads

Cook over boiling water, stirring constantly until mixture thickens. Add gelatine soaked in cold water. Strain and add to salmon. Fill mold or molds with mixture. Chill, remove from molds to bed of lettuce leaves, and serve with

### CUCUMBER SAUCE

Beat one-half cup heavy cream until stiff, add one-fourth teaspoon salt, a few grains pepper, and gradually two tablespoons vinegar; then add one cucumber pared, chopped, and drained.

### FAIRMONT SANDWICHES

Cut white bread in one-fourth inch slices and spread two of the slices sparingly on both sides with butter worked until creamy; spread remaining two slices on but one side. Put between slices layers of finely chopped red or green peppers (wrung in cheese-cloth to remove all possible moisture) moistened with Mayonnaise dressing. There should be two layers of green peppers and one of red, or just the reverse. Repeat until a sufficient quantity are prepared. Fold in cheese-cloth and press under a light weight. Cut in one-fourth inch slices and arrange overlapping one another, in two or three rows, on a plate covered with a doiley.

## Washington's Birthday Spreads

### ALMOND CREAM

1 pint thin cream
¾ cup blanched and shredded almonds
Yolks 3 eggs
½ cup sugar
⅛ teaspoon salt
1½ tablespoons granulated gelatine
½ cup cold water
½ teaspoon vanilla
1 cup heavy cream

Scald milk with almonds. Beat yolks of eggs slightly and add sugar and salt. Combine mixtures and cook in double boiler, stirring constantly until mixture thickens. Add gelatine soaked in cold water. Cool slightly and add vanilla, and cut and fold in cream, beaten until stiff. Turn into a border mold and chill. Remove from mold to serving dish and fill centre with wine jelly cut in cubes or beaten with a fork until frothy, and garnish with candied cherries.

### WINE JELLY

2 tablespoons granulated gelatine
½ cup cold water
1⅔ cups boiling water
1 cup sugar
1 cup Sherry or Madeira wine
⅓ cup orange juice
3 tablespoons lemon juice

Soak gelatine in cold water, dissolve in boiling water; add sugar, wine, orange juice, and lemon juice, strain, turn into a mold or shallow pan, and chill.

## 58  Washington's Birthday Spreads

### PEANUT DROPS

2 tablespoons butter
¼ cup sugar
1 egg
1 teaspoon baking powder
¼ teaspoon salt
½ cup flour
2 tablespoons milk
½ cup finely chopped peanuts

Cream the butter, add sugar, and egg well beaten. Mix and sift baking powder, salt, and flour; add to first mixture, then add milk and peanuts. Drop from a teaspoon on a slightly buttered sheet one inch apart, and place one-half peanut on top of each. Bake twelve to fifteen minutes in a slow oven. This recipe will make twenty-four little cakes.

### GEORGE WASHINGTON HATCHETS

Mix and sift two cups flour and one-half cup brown sugar. Wash three-fourths cup butter and work into first mixture, using tips of fingers. Roll to one-third inch in thickness and cut into hatchet shapes, which can be easily accomplished with a pasteboard pattern and sharp knife. Brush over with yolk of egg diluted with three-fourths teaspoon water, and garnish each with one-half a candied cherry  Bake in a slow oven.

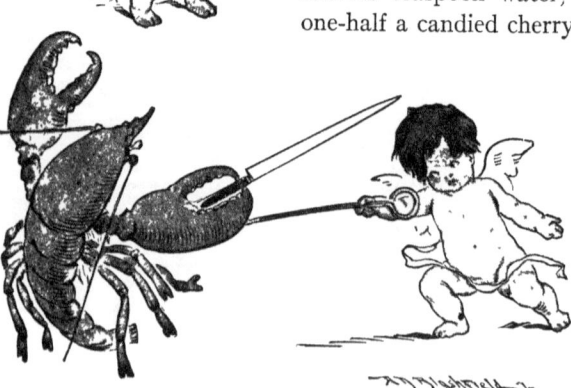

## Washington's Birthday Spreads

### FRUIT PUNCH

| | |
|---|---|
| 1 cup sugar | ⅓ cup lemon juice |
| 1 cup hot tea infusion | 1 pint ginger ale |
| ¾ cup orange juice | 1 pint Lithia water |
| Few slices orange | Maraschino cherries |

Pour tea over sugar, and as soon as sugar is dissolved add fruit juices. Strain into punch bowl over a large piece of ice, and just before serving add ale, Lithia, slices of orange, and cherries.

# Washington's Birthday Spreads

## MENU NO. II.

*"Superfluous compliments and all affectation of ceremony are to be avoided, yet where due they are not to be neglected."*
From George Washington's Note Book.

Shapleigh Croquettes

Cherry Salad

**Layer** Sandwiches

Sedalia Sticks

Apricot Bombe

Oat Wafers

Quality Cake

Knickerbocker Figs

62    Washington's Birthday Spreads

## SHAPLEIGH CROQUETTES

3 tablespoons butter
¼ tablespoon finely chopped onion
¼ cup flour
1 cup chicken stock
1 teaspoon salt
¼ teaspoon paprika
⅛ teaspoon pepper
Few gratings nutmeg
Yolks 3 eggs
1¼ cups chicken, cut in small cubes
½ cup cold boiled ham, cut in small cubes

Cook butter with onion three minutes, stirring constantly. Add flour and stir until well blended; then pour on gradually, while stirring constantly, chicken stock. Bring to the boiling-point and add seasonings, yolks of eggs slightly beaten, chicken, and ham. Spread on a plate to cool. Shape, dip in crumbs, egg and crumbs, fry in deep fat, and drain on brown paper. Remove to hot serving dish and garnish with parsley.

## CHERRY SALAD

Drain canned cherries, remove stones, and fill cavities with filbert nut meats. Arrange in nests of lettuce leaves and serve with Cream Mayonnaise Dressing.

## LAYER SANDWICHES

Cut brown and white bread in thin slices and spread with creamed butter. Cut tongue and

## Washington's Birthday Spreads

gruyère cheese in slices. Arrange sliced tongue over the white bread, and over tongue brown bread, and over brown bread cheese, repeat, trim evenly, put under a weight and let stand for several hours, then cut crosswise in thin slices. Arrange on a plate covered with a doiley, overlapping one another.

### SEDALIA STICKS

Mix one-fourth cup each finely chopped preserved Canton ginger and chopped pecan nut meats. Add two tablespoons finely cut candied orange peel, one tablespoon ginger syrup, one teaspoon vinegar, and a few grains salt. Spread between saltines or slices of thinly buttered bread. Arrange on a plate covered with a doiley.

### CANDIED ORANGE PEEL

Remove peel from four thin-skinned oranges in quarters. Cover with cold water, bring to boiling-point, and cook slowly until soft. Drain, remove white portion by scraping with a spoon, and cut yellow portion in thin strips, using scissors. Boil one-half cup water and one cup sugar until syrup will thread when dropped from tip of spoon. Cook strips in syrup five minutes, drain, and coat with fine granulated sugar.

## 64  Washington's Birthday Spreads

### APRICOT BOMBE

| | |
|---|---|
| 1 can apricots | ¼ cup lemon juice |
| 1½ cups orange juice | A few grains salt |
| Sugar | |

Drain apricots and force through a purée strainer. To the syrup add fruit juices, salt, and apricot purée; then sweeten to taste. Freeze, using three parts finely crushed ice to one part rock salt. Line a melon mold with mixture, fill with Praline Ice Cream. Cover ice cream with apricot mixture to overflow mold, adjust cover, pack in salt and ice, using equal parts, and let stand three hours.

### PRALINE ICE CREAM

| | |
|---|---|
| 1 cup sugar | Yolks 3 eggs |
| ⅔ cup pecan nut meats | Few grains salt |
| 2 cups scalded milk | 1 cup heavy cream |
| ¾ tablespoon vanilla | |

Put one-half the sugar in a small omelet pan, and stir constantly until melted to a syrup a bit darker than maple syrup. Add chopped nut meats and turn into a slightly buttered tin. Cool, pound, and pass through a strainer. Make a custard of milk, eggs, remaining sugar, and salt. Add nut meats and cool, then add cream and vanilla. Freeze, using three parts finely crushed ice to one part rock salt.

# Washington's Birthday Spreads

## OAT WAFERS

1 egg
½ cup sugar
⅔ tablespoon melted butter
⅓ teaspoon salt
¾ cup rolled oats
¼ cup raisins, seeded and cut in pieces
¼ teaspoon vanilla

Beat egg until light, add sugar gradually, and then stir in remaining ingredients. Drop mixture by teaspoonfuls on a thoroughly greased inverted dripping-pan one inch apart. Spread into circular shape with a case knife first dipped in cold water. Bake in a moderate oven until delicately browned.

## QUALITY CAKE

½ cup butter
1½ cups sugar
5 eggs
2⅓ cups flour
2½ teaspoons baking powder
½ cup milk

Cream butter and add sugar gradually while beating constantly; then add eggs beaten until thick. Mix and sift flour and baking powder, and add alternately with milk to first mixture. Turn into buttered and floured layer cake tins and bake in a moderate oven. Put together and frost with

## 66   Washington's Birthday Spreads

### QUALITY FROSTING

2 cups sugar
3 tablespoons molasses
½ cup water
Whites 2 eggs

⅔ teaspoon vanilla
⅓ teaspoon lemon
1 cup nut meats
Few grains salt

Cook sugar, molasses, and water until mixture will nearly hold its shape when tried in cold water. Pour slowly while beating constantly on to the whites of eggs beaten stiff. Put saucepan in larger saucepan of boiling water, set on range, and stir constantly until mixture begins to granulate on sides of saucepan. Remove small saucepan and beat until mixture is of right consistency to spread, then add flavoring and nut meats (preferably filberts) cut in small pieces. This makes a heavy, soft frosting, which should be spread with back of spoon, leaving a rough surface.

### KNICKERBOCKER FIGS

½ lb. washed figs
Maraschino cherries
Pecan nut meats

2 tablespoons sugar
1 teaspoon lemon juice
½ cup sherry wine

Stuff figs with cherries and nut meats, allowing two cherries and three nut meats cut in quarters to each fig. Mix remaining ingredients. Add

## Washington's Birthday Spreads 67

figs, cover, and cook until figs are tender, turning and basting several times during the cooking. Remove to board, roll in powdered sugar, and place in individual paper cases if they are at hand. Arrange on a plate covered with a lace paper doiley.

A ST. PATRICK'S DAY LUNCHEON.

## ST. PATRICK'S DAY LUNCHEONS

## St. Patrick's Day Luncheons

### MENU NO I.

*"We shall
Do nothing but eat and make good cheer."*
    Shakspere.

Oyster Cocktail

St. Patrick's Soup    Crisp Crackers

Haddon Hall Halibut    Rolls

Tournados of Beef    Batonet Potatoes

Soubrics of Spinach

Cork Timbales

Shamrock Salad    Cheese Cakes

Irish Iceberg    Rolled Wafers

Café Noir

72    St. Patrick's Day Luncheons

### OYSTER COCKTAIL

Allow seven Blue Point oysters to each person, and season with three-fourths tablespoon lemon-juice, one-half tablespoon tomato catsup, one-half teaspoon finely chopped shallot, three drops Tobasco sauce, and salt to taste. Chill thoroughly and serve in cocktail glasses. Sprinkle with finely chopped celery and garnish with small pieces green pepper.

### ST. PATRICK'S SOUP

| | |
|---|---|
| 3 potatoes | 1½ teaspoons salt |
| 1 quart milk | ¼ teaspoon celery salt |
| 2 slices onion | ⅛ teaspoon pepper |
| 3 tablespoons butter | Few grains cayenne |
| 2 tablespoons flour | 3 tablespoons tomato catsup |
| 1 teaspoon chopped parsley | |

Cook potatoes in boiling salted water; when soft, rub through a strainer. Scald milk with onion, remove onion, and add milk slowly to potatoes  Melt half the butter, add dry ingredients, stir until well mixed, then stir into boiling soup; cook one minute, strain, add remaining butter and tomato catsup, and sprinkle with parsley.   Serve in bouillon cups.

# St. Patrick's Day Luncheons

### CRISP CRACKERS

Split common crackers and spread with butter, using one-fourth teaspoon butter to each one-half cracker. Place in pan and bake in a moderate oven until delicately browned.

### HADDON HALL HALIBUT

Wipe two slices chicken halibut, each weighing three-fourths pound, and cut into eight fillets. Sprinkle with salt and lemon juice, roll, fasten with small wooden skewers (tooth-picks), cover, and let stand thirty minutes. Cook over boiling salted water, remove to individual fish plates, pour around mushroom sauce, and place a selected sauted mushroom cap on each.

### MUSHROOM SAUCE

Melt three tablespoons butter, add three tablespoons flour, and stir until well blended; then pour on gradually, while stirring constantly, one cup fish stock and one-half cup cream. When boiling-point is reached, add one tablespoon Sauterne wine, three sliced mushroom caps, one-half teaspoon salt, and a few grains pepper. Let simmer until caps are soft.

To obtain fish stock, cover bones, skin, and trimming of fish with cold water; bring slowly

74  St. Patrick's Day Luncheons

to the boiling-point and let simmer until reduced to one cup.

### TOURNADOS OF BEEF

Wipe six small fillets of beef, cut one and one-fourth inches thick, and sauté six minutes in butter in a hot iron frying pan. Remove to hot serving dish and pour around fat in pan to which have been added one-fourth cup boiling water, one-half teaspoon beef extract, and one tablespoon butter, bit by bit. Garnish with parsley.

### BATONET POTATOES

Wash and pare potatoes. With a French vegetable cutter shape in pieces three inches long and one-half inch in diameter. Fry in deep fat, drain on brown paper, and sprinkle with salt.

### SOUBRICS OF SPINACH

Thoroughly wash two quarts spinach, boil, drain, and chop. Add two tablespoons grated Parmesan cheese and the yolk of one egg slightly beaten. Season with salt, cayenne, and a slight grating nutmeg and cook three minutes, stirring constantly; then add the white of one egg beaten slightly. Measure by rounding tablespoonfuls and sauté in butter. Serve with a white sauce.

## St. Patrick's Day Luncheons

### CORK TIMBALES

Line the sides of buttered timbale molds with green pepper cut in thin strips, which is accomplished by working around and around the pepper, using scissors, and fill with the following mixture: Peel and chop three large mushroom caps. Melt one tablespoon butter, and add one tablespoon flour, and one-fourth cup cream. Beat in, one at a time, the yolks of two eggs, then add mushrooms and season with salt, pepper, and paprika. Fold in the whites of two eggs beaten until stiff. Bake timbales, remove from molds to circular pieces of sautéd bread, garnish top of each with a sautéd mushroom cap, and pour around the following sauce: Melt two tablespoons butter, add two tablespoons flour, and pour on gradually one-half cup each chicken stock and cream. Bring to the boiling-point and add one-half teaspoon beef extract and season with salt and pepper.

### SHAMROCK SALAD

Pare cucumbers and cut in rectangular, box-shaped pieces two and three-fourths inches long by one and one-half inches high (being careful to keep all the angles right angles), then cut in thin slices, keeping sections in original shape. Spread evenly and smoothly with Mayonnaise

dressing (stiffening one cup with one-half teaspoon granulated gelatin dissolved in one-half tablespoon hot water) and garnish in centre with small pieces of green pepper cut to represent a shamrock; in corners with diamond-shaped pieces of truffle. A small wooden skewer (tooth-pick) is useful to accomplish this garnishing. Serve individually in nests of lettuce leaves.

### CHEESE CAKES

| | |
|---|---|
| 2 tablespoons butter | Whites 3 eggs |
| 3½ tablespoons flour | ¼ teaspoon salt |
| 4 tablespoons grated American cheese | Few grains cayenne |

Melt butter, add flour, and stir until well blended; then add cheese and cut and fold in whites of eggs beaten until stiff. Season with salt and cayenne. Drop from tip of spoon on a buttered sheet one inch apart and bake in a moderate oven.

### IRISH ICEBERG

| | |
|---|---|
| 4 cups water | Green coloring |
| 2 cups sugar | Crême de menthe |
| ¾ cup lemon juice | Chopped nuts |

Make a syrup by boiling water and sugar twenty minutes. Cool, add lemon juice, and color with leaf green. Freeze, using three pints finely crushed ice to one pint rock salt.

## St. Patrick's Day Luncheons

Serve in champagne glasses; pour over each portion one teaspoon crême de menthe and sprinkle with chopped nuts, using almonds, walnuts, and pecans in equal proportions.

### ROLLED WAFERS

¼ cup butter  
½ cup powdered sugar  
¾ teaspoon vanilla  
¼ cup milk  
⅞ cup bread flour  
¼ teaspoon almond extract  
Leaf green  
Chopped pistachio nuts

Cream the butter, add sugar gradually, and milk drop by drop, then add flour, flavoring, and coloring. Spread very thinly with a broad, long-bladed knife on a buttered inverted dripping-pan. Crease in three-inch squares and bake in a slow oven. Place pan on back of range, cut squares apart with a sharp knife, and roll while warm. If squares become too brittle to roll, place in oven to soften. If rolled tubular shape, tie in bunches with narrow ribbon. Colored wafers must be baked in a very slow oven and turned frequently, otherwise they will not be of the uniform color that is desired.

## MENU NO. II.

*" The name that dwells on every tongue
No minstrel needs."*

Shamrock Canapes

Spinach Soup     Imperial Sticks

Fillets of Halibut, Loomis     Cole Slaw

Kernels of Pork     Savory Potatoes

Stuffed Onions

Malaga Salad

Pistachio Ice Cream, Peach Sauce     Condés

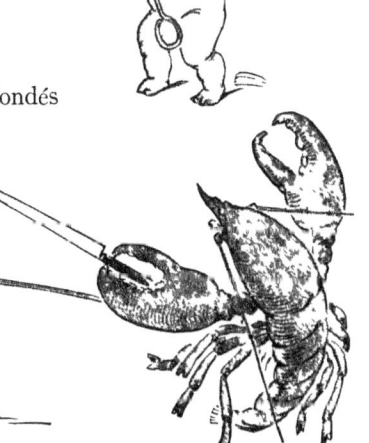

# 80  St. Patrick's Day Luncheons

## SHAMROCK CANAPES

Force cream cake mixture through a pastry bag and tube in small groups of threes, which when baked make shamrock forms. Split and fill with the following mixture: Pound six sardines, freed from skin and bones, and add one and one-half tablespoons butter worked until creamy, and two tablespoons Anchovy paste. Season with salt, cayenne, and lemon juice.

Arrange for service on small individual plates covered with lace paper doilies and garnish with watercress.

## SPINACH SOUP

| | |
|---|---|
| 4 cups chicken stock | ¼ cup butter |
| 2 quarts spinach | ⅓ cup flour |
| 3 cups boiling water | Salt |
| 2 cups milk | Pepper |
| Paprika | |

Wash, pick over, and cook spinach thirty minutes in boiling water to which have been added one-fourth teaspoon powdered sugar and one-eighth teaspoon of soda; drain, chop, and rub through sieve; add stock, heat to boiling-point, bind with butter and flour cooked together, add milk, and season with salt, pepper, and paprika.

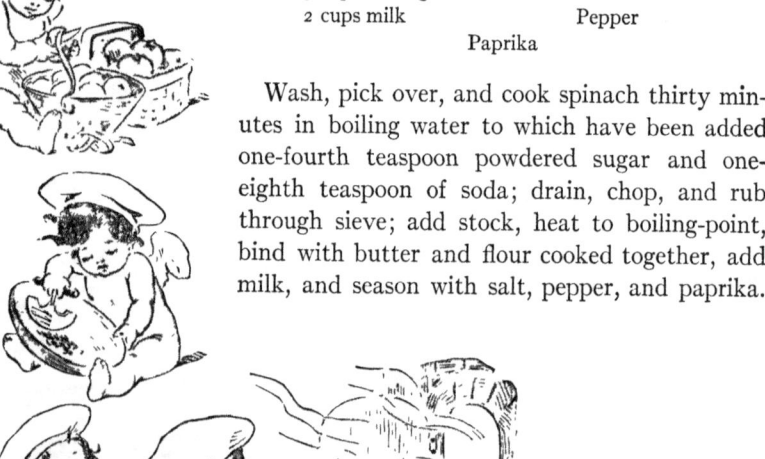

## St. Patrick's Day Luncheons

### IMPERIAL STICKS

Cut stale bread in one-third-inch slices, remove crusts, butter sparingly, and cut in one-third-inch strips. Place in pan and bake in a moderate oven until delicately browned.

Cut stale bread in slices, shape with circular cutters, making rings. Spread rings sparingly with butter and brown in oven. Slip three imperial sticks through each ring.

### FILLETS OF HALIBUT, LOOMIS

| | |
|---|---|
| 2 ¾ lb. slices halibut | 2 cloves |
| 1 onion, sliced | ½ cup white wine |
| 8 slices carrot | Cold water |
| 2 sprigs parsley | Salt |
| 1 sprig thyme | Pepper |
| Bit bay leaf | Vinegar |

Wipe fish, cut into eight fillets, and arrange in pan. Lay vegetables over fish, pour over wine, and add water to cover fish; then sprinkle with salt and pepper and add vinegar. Cover and let stand two hours. Put on range, bring to boiling-point, and let boil until fish is soft. Remove to hot platter, pour over Loomis Sauce, sprinkle with two tablespoons grated Parmesan cheese, dot over with one tablespoon butter, and bake until delicately browned.

## LOOMIS SAUCE

| | |
|---|---|
| 2 tablespoons butter | ⅓ cup fish liquor |
| 3 tablespoons flour | 2 tablespoons grated |
| ½ cup milk | mild cheese |
| Yolk 1 egg | Salt and cayenne |

Melt butter, add flour, and stir until well blended; then pour on gradually while stirring constantly milk and fish stock. Bring to the boiling-point, add cheese and egg yolk slightly beaten, and season with salt and cayenne.

To obtain fish liquor, cover bones, skin, and trimmings of fish with cold water. Cover and let stand one-half hour. Bring to boiling-point and let simmer until liquor is reduced to one-third cup.

## COLE SLAW

Select a small, heavy cabbage, take off outside leaves, and cut in quarters; with a sharp knife slice very thinly. Soak in cold water until crisp, drain, dry between towels, and mix with Cream Dressing.

## CREAM DRESSING

| | |
|---|---|
| ½ tablespoon salt | 1 egg slightly beaten |
| ½ tablespoon mustard | 2½ tablespoons melted |
| ¾ tablespoon sugar | butter |
| ¼ cup vinegar | ¾ cup cream |

## St. Patrick's Day Luncheons

Mix ingredients in order given, adding vinegar very slowly. Cook over boiling water, stirring constantly until mixture thickens, strain, and cool.

### KERNELS OF PORK

Cut lean meat from a spare rib of pork; then cut in three-fourth-inch slices and cook in a hissing hot iron frying pan which has been rubbed over with fat pork

Arrange in a row lengthwise of a hot platter, and on sides of platter pile Savory Potatoes and garnish with parsley.

### SAVORY POTATOES

To two cups hot riced potatoes add three tablespoons butter, one teaspoon salt, and hot cream or rich milk to moisten. Beat until very creamy, reheat, and add one tablespoon chopped watercress and one and one-half teaspoons chopped fresh mint.

### STUFFED ONIONS

Peel six large Bermuda onions and remove a part of inside. Cover with boiling water and cook five minutes; drain and stuff. Place in a baking dish on six thin slices fat salt pork, pour over one cup brown stock and bake in a moderate oven until onions are soft. Remove to hot

plates on circular pieces of sautéd bread. Strain liquor remaining in pan, remove fat, and add one teaspoon beef extract and one-half tablespoon butter. Season with salt and pepper and pour over onions.

For the stuffing, cook one tablespoon butter with one tablespoon finely chopped onion three minutes. Add one-half cup soft bread crumbs, one-half cup finely chopped raw veal, and two tablespoons finely chopped salt pork. Season with one-half teaspoon salt and a few grains pepper; then add one egg slightly beaten.

### MALAGA SALAD

Mix one-half cup shredded pineapple, one-half cup celery cut in small pieces, and one-half cup Brazil nuts (from which skins have been removed) cut in small pieces.

Mix with Mayonnaise dressing, arrange in nests of lettuce leaves for individual service, and on top of each put five Malaga grapes, skinned, seeded, and marinated with a French dressing.

### PISTACHIO ICE CREAM, PEACH SAUCE

| | |
|---|---|
| 4 cups lukewarm milk | 1 tablespoon cold water |
| 1 cup heavy cream | 1 tablespoon vanilla |
| 1¼ cups sugar | 1 teaspoon almond extract |
| ⅛ teaspoon salt | Green coloring |
| 1½ Junket tablets | 1 can peaches |

## St. Patrick's Day Luncheons 85

Mix first four ingredients and add junket tablets dissolved in cold water. Turn into a pudding-dish and let stand until set. Add flavoring and coloring. Freeze and mold Remove from mold and serve with peach sauce.

Turn peaches into a saucepan, add one-third cup sugar, and cook slowly until syrup is thick. Cool and cut fruit in small pieces.

### CONDÉS

Whites 2 eggs  2 oz. almonds, blanched
¼ cup powdered sugar  and finely chopped

Beat whites of eggs until stiff and add sugar gradually, while beating constantly; then add almonds. Roll paste, and cut in strips three and one-half inches long by one and one-half inches wide. Spread with mixture; avoid having it come close to edge. Dust with powdered sugar and bake fifteen minutes in moderate oven.

AN EASTER DINNER TABLE.

# EASTER DINNERS

Easter Dinners

## MENU NO. I.

*"How beat our hearts big with tumultuous joy!"*

Dexter Canapes

Mushroom Soup

Perch Britannia        Finger Sticks

Ambassadrice Capon with Asparagus

Anchovied Potatoes in Shells

Crab Meat Mornay      Easter Salad

Piquante Mayonnaise     Chantilly Moussé

Salted Nuts    Cream Mints    Preserved Ginger

Café Noir

## Easter Dinners

### DEXTER CANAPES

Cut stale bread in one-fourth-inch slices, then in oval shapes. Toast on one side and spread untoasted side with anchovy butter. Cover each with a slice of tomato, cut same size as bread, spread tomato with mayonnaise dressing, sprinkle with the yolks of hard-boiled eggs forced through a potato ricer, and then the whites finely chopped. Garnish with a ring of green pepper around outside and a piece of olive and parsley in centre. Arrange for individual service on small plates covered with a lace paper doiley.

### MUSHROOM SOUP

½ lb. mushrooms     3 pints consommé

Separate stems from caps of mushrooms, chop stems, and break caps in pieces. Add consommé; bring slowly to the boiling-point and let simmer thirty minutes. Clear, using the whites and shells of two eggs.

### PERCH BRITANNIA

Clean fish, remove heads, tails, and back-bones, and cut in one-inch pieces crosswise. Cut thin slices of bacon same size as pieces of perch. Arrange fish and bacon alternately on skewers,

## Easter Dinners

having four of each. Brush over with olive oil mixed with salt and pepper, roll in crumbs, fry in deep fat, and drain on brown paper. Serve with sections of lemon.

### FINGER STICKS

½ cup cream  
2 tablespoons sugar  
¼ teaspoon salt  
1 yeast cake dissolved in ¼ cup lukewarm water  
1½ cups flour

Scald cream and add sugar and salt. When lukewarm, add dissolved yeast cake and flour. Beat thoroughly, toss on floured board, and knead. Return to mixing bowl, cover, and let rise until mixture has doubled its bulk. Roll out to one-fourth inch in thickness and cut in finger-shaped pieces. Arrange on buttered sheet, cover again, let rise, and bake until delicately browned. Brush over with two tablespoons milk, and return to oven for one minute.

### AMBASSADRICE CAPON WITH ASPARAGUS

Dress, clean, stuff, truss, and roast a capon. Cut a slice in such fashion as to remove wishbone, not quite cutting off; then cut around second joints at body, also not cutting off, and force wings back. Cut breast meat in slices. Cut as many one-third inch slices of bread as there are

slices of breast meat and shape in cutlet form. spread one side with paté-de-fois-gras and sauté in butter.

Arrange around bird, place breast meat on croutons, and garnish top of each with truffle. With a sharp knife cut out breast bone and fill cavity with cooked asparagus tips or stalks, seasoned with butter and salt. Garnish with parsley and serve with a gravy made from four tablespoons fat remaining in pan, four tablespoons flour, one cup each chicken stock and cream, and salt and pepper.

### ANCHOVIED POTATOES IN SHELLS

Wash and peel six medium-sized potatoes and bake, turning frequently. Cut a thin slice from each and scoop out inside, then force through a ricer. Season with two tablespoons butter, twelve anchovies cut in small pieces, one-eighth teaspoon nutmeg, and two-thirds cup hot milk. Season with salt and pepper, refill shells, dot over with butter, and brown in a moderate oven.

### CRAB MEAT MORNAY

4½ tablespoons butter     ¾ cup chicken stock
3 tablespoons flour     ½ teaspoon salt
2½ tablespoons cornstarch     Yolks of 2 eggs
¾ cup milk     1½ cups crab meat
Grated Young America Cheese

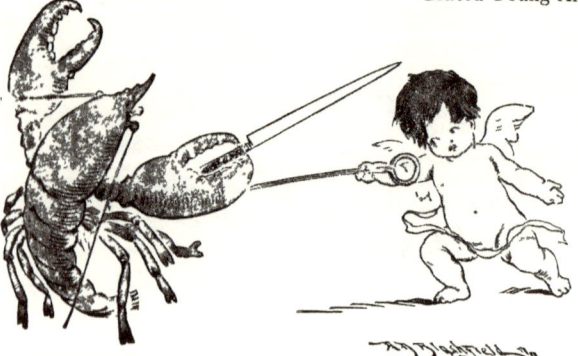

Easter Dinners

Melt butter, add flour, cornstarch, and salt. Pour on gradually, while stirring constantly, milk and chicken stock. Bring to the boiling-point, add salt, and let simmer two minutes, then add yolks of eggs. Butter eight individual casseroles, cover bottoms with crab meat, then cover with sauce. Sprinkle with cheese and run under the gas flame to brown.

### EASTER SALAD

Put eggs in top of double boiler, cover with boiling water, put over under part of double boiler which contains boiling water, cover, and let cook on range thirty-five minutes. Remove shells, and while hot hold between thumb and finger while pressing into apple shapes. Mix a bit of fruit red with cold water and brush over eggs with mixture. Insert clove to represent blossom end, a stem and leaves (hot-house lilac leaves answer the purpose) to represent stem, and serve on lettuce leaves with

### MAYONNAISE PIQUANTE

To one cup mayonnaise dressing add two tablespoons each olives and pickles, finely chopped.

## MAYONNAISE DRESSING

| | |
|---|---|
| 1 teaspoon mustard | Yolks 2 eggs |
| 1 teaspoon salt | 2 tablespoons lemon juice |
| 1 teaspoon powdered sugar | 2 tablespoons vinegar |
| Few grains cayenne | 1½ cups olive oil |

Mix dry ingredients, add egg yolks, and when well mixed add one-half teaspoon of vinegar. Add oil gradually, at first drop by drop, and stir constantly. As mixture thickens, thin with vinegar or lemon juice. Add oil and vinegar or lemon juice alternately until all is used, stirring or beating constantly. If oil is added too rapidly, dressing will have a curdled appearance. A smooth consistency may be restored by taking yolk of another egg and adding curdled mixture slowly to it. It is desirable to have bowl containing mixture placed in a larger bowl of crushed ice, to which a small quantity of water has been added. Olive oil for making mayonnaise should always be thoroughly chilled. A silver fork, wire whisk, small wooden spoon, or Dover Egg-beater may be used, as preferred.

## CHANTILLY MOUSSÉ

| | |
|---|---|
| 1 pint heavy cream | Few grains salt |
| ½ cup sugar | 10 drops Hundt's |
| 2 cups meringues, broken in pieces | essence of violets |

## Easter Dinners

Beat cream until stiff, using a Dover Eggbeater, and add sugar, salt, essence of violet, and meringues. Pack in salt and ice, using equal parts, and let stand four hours. Remove to serving-dish and garnish with candied violets, angelica, and a bunch of fresh violets.

### MERINGUES

Whites 4 eggs     1 cup fine granulated sugar
½ teaspoon vanilla

Beat whites of eggs until stiff and add gradually, while beating constantly, two-thirds cup sugar. Fold in one-third cup sugar and add one-half teaspoon vanilla. Shape with spoon on tin sheet covered with letter paper and bake thirty minutes in slow oven.

Easter Dinners. 97

MENU NO. II.

*"Hospitality must be for service, not for show, or it pulls down the hostess."*
                                                    Emerson.

Rector Canapes

Pimiento Bisque          Souffléd Crackers

   Halibut au Lit        Cucumber Ribbons

Crown of Lamb            Currant Mint Sauce

Potatoes Rissolées     Glazed Carrots with Peas

      Sweetbreads à la Huntington

Malaga Salad    Entire Wheat Bread Sandwiches

   Wordsworth Pudding     Mock Macaroons

         Mint Paste

   Crackers              Cheese

            Café Noir

## Easter Dinners

### RECTOR CANAPES

Cut bread in one-fourth-inch slices, then in strips three and one-half inches long by one and one-half inches wide. Toast slightly on one side and spread untoasted side with caviare. Decorate each with two fillets of anchovies, placed from opposite corners diagonally on strips. Between anchovies sprinkle finely chopped pickles and in each corner finely chopped olives.

### PIMIENTO BISQUE

3 pints chicken stock  1 teaspoon salt
½ cup rice  ½ cup cream
4 canned pimientos  Yolks 2 eggs

Cook rice in double boiler with stock until tender. Rub through a sieve and add pimientos, also rubbed through a sieve. Bring to the boiling-point, add salt, and cream mixed with the yolks of eggs, slightly beaten.

### SOUFFLÉD CRACKERS

Split common crackers and soak in ice-water, to cover, eight minutes. Drain, arrange in baking pan, and drop one-third teaspoon butter in centre of each. Bake in a hot oven until puffed and browned, the time required being about forty minutes.

## Easter Dinners

### HALIBUT AU LIT

Wipe a slice chicken halibut and cut in eight fillets. Sprinkle with salt and lemon juice, roll, and fasten with small wooden skewers. Cook over boiling water until tender. Arrange a steamed fillet in the centre of each fish plate, and place on top of each a cooked mushroom cap. Serve with mushroom sauce and garnish each with watercress and radish cut in fancy shape.

### MUSHROOM SAUCE

Melt three tablespoons butter, add three tablespoons flour, and pour on gradually, while stirring constantly, one cup fish stock. When boiling-point is reached add one-half cup cream, three mushroom caps, sliced, and one tablespoon sauterne. Season with salt and pepper. The fish stock should be made from skin and bones of halibut. The mushroom caps on fillets should be cooked in sauce till soft.

### CUCUMBER RIBBONS

Cut a thick slice from both ends of cucumbers and pare; then cut in one-fourth-inch slices. Cut slices round and round to form ribbons, using a small sharp knife. Plunge into cold water and let stand one-half hour. Drain, sprinkle with salt, and pour over vinegar.

## Easter Dinners

### ROAST CROWN OF LAMB

Select parts from two loins containing ribs, scrape flesh from bone between ribs, as far as lean meat, and trim off backbone. Shape each piece in a semicircle, having ribs outside, and sew pieces together to form a crown. This work may be done at any first-class market. Trim ends of bones evenly, care being taken that they are not left too long, and wrap each bone in a thin strip of fat salt pork or insert ends in cubes of fat salt pork to prevent bone from burning, then cover with buttered paper. Roast one and one-fourth hours, basting frequently. Remove to hot platter, take off pork, and fill centre with glazed carrots and peas. Garnish with parsley. Accompany with

### CURRANT MINT SAUCE

Separate two-thirds tumbler of currant jelly in pieces, but do not beat it. Add one and one-half tablespoons finely chopped mint leaves and shavings from the rind of one-fourth orange.

### GLAZED CARROTS WITH PEAS

Wash and scrape carrots, then cut in strips; there should be four cups. Cook in boiling salted water to cover fifteen minutes, drain, and return to saucepan with one-half cup butter and one-

half tablespoon sugar. Cover and cook very slowly until tender. Add one can French peas, drained, cooked in boiling water ten minutes, then seasoned with butter, salt, and pepper.

### POTATOES RISSOLÉES

Wash, pare, and trim new potatoes in egg shapes. Let stand in cold water fifteen minutes, dry thoroughly, and fry in deep fat until delicately browned. Drain and bake from twenty to twenty-five minutes or until potatoes are soft. Serve with

### CREAM SAUCE

Melt two tablespoons butter, add two tablespoons flour and stir until well blended, then pour on gradually while beating constantly one cup cream. Bring to the boiling-point and season with salt and pepper.

### SWEETBREADS À LA HUNTINGTON

Parboil a large sweetbread and cut in eight pieces. Cook in hot frying-pan with a small quantity of butter, adding enough beef extract to give sweetbread a glazed appearance. Cut bread in slices, shape with a circular cutter three and one-half inches in diameter, and toast. Spread each piece with two tablespoons grated

Parmesan cheese seasoned with salt and paprika. Put in a buttered shallow pan and pour over cream, allowing three tablespoons to each piece of bread. Arrange one piece of sweetbread on each piece of toast. Cover each sweetbread with three sautéd mushroom caps and bake in a moderate oven five minutes, covering pan with a piece of glass.

## MALAGA SALAD

Seed and peel white grapes and stuff with canned pimientos. Separate tangerines into sections and free from skin and seed. Mash a small cream cheese, moisten with French dressing, add one-fourth cup chopped pecan nut meats, and make into balls size of grapes. Arrange all on nests of lettuce leaves for individual service and serve with French dressing.

## ENTIRE WHEAT BREAD

2 cups scalded milk    1 teaspoon salt
¼ cup sugar    1 yeast cake dissolved in
⅓ cup molasses      ¼ cup lukewarm water
     4⅔ cups coarse entire wheat flour

Add sweetening and salt to milk, cool, and when lukewarm add dissolved yeast cake and flour. beat well, cover, and let rise to double its bulk; Again beat, and turn into greased bread pans, having pans one-half full; let rise and bake.

## Easter Dinners

### ENTIRE WHEAT BREAD SANDWICHES

Spread thin slices of entire wheat bread with creamed butter, put together in pairs, remove crusts, cut in any desired shapes, and pile on a plate covered with a doiley.

### WADSWORTH PUDDING

| | |
|---|---|
| 2 cups thin cream | Whites 4 eggs |
| 1½ tablespoons granulated gelatine | 3 tablespoons sherry |
| | 1½ tablespoons sauterne |
| 2 tablespoons cold water | ¾ cup sugar |

Scald cream, add gelatine soaked in cold water, then add whites of eggs beaten until stiff; add sugar. Remove from range, set in pan of ice-water, and stir occasionally until mixture thickens, then add flavoring and turn into mold. Chill thoroughly, remove from mold, and surround with cubes of orange jelly.

### ORANGE JELLY

| | |
|---|---|
| ½ box gelatine or | 1½ cups boiling water |
| 2 tablespoons granulated gelatine | 1 cup sugar |
| | 1½ cups orange juice |
| ½ cup cold water | 3 tablespoons lemon juice |

Soak gelatine in cold water, dissolve in boiling water, strain, and add to sugar and fruit juices. Turn into a shallow pan, chill thoroughly, and cut into cubes.

## MOCK MACAROONS

| White 1 egg | 1 cup pecan nut meats |
| 1 cup brown sugar | ¼ teaspoon salt |

Beat white of egg until light, using a Dover egg-beater, and add gradually, while beating constantly, sugar  Cut and fold in the nuts finely chopped and sprinkled with salt. Drop from tip of spoon, one inch apart, on a buttered sheet, and bake eight minutes in a moderate oven. This recipe makes twenty-four little cakes.

## MINT PASTE

Soak three tablespoons granulated gelatine in one-half cup cold water thirty minutes. To two cups sugar add one-half cup cold water, and bring to the boiling-point, then add the gelatine and let boil twenty minutes. Remove from fire and add two tablespoons lemon juice, four tablespoons crème de menthe, and a few grains salt. Pour into a pan and let stand until stiff; then remove from pan, cut in cubes, and roll in confectioners' sugar.

FOURTH OF JULY RECEPTION TABLE.

# FOURTH OF JULY SPREADS

Fourth of July Spreads 107

MENU No. I

*"The man's the best cosmopolite
Who loves his native country best."*
                    Tennyson.

Iced Tomato Bouillon

Salmon Balls          Sweetbread Salad

   Lenox Sandwiches     Salad Rolls

      Strawberry Biscuit Macaroon

Cocoanut Rings      Lady Baltimore Cake

       Fourth of July Punch

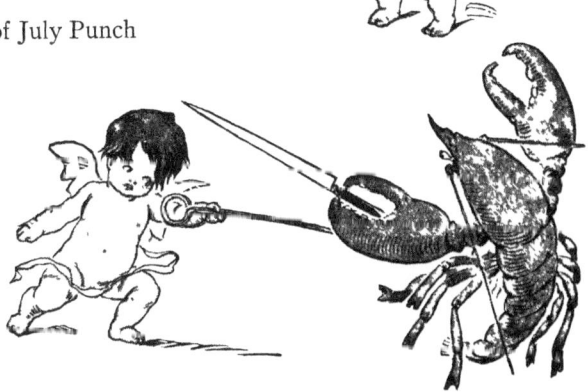

## Fourth of July Spreads

### ICED TOMATO BOUILLON

| | |
|---|---|
| 3½ lbs. lean beef from round | 2 tablespoons butter |
| 2 lbs marrow-bone | Carrot } ⅓ cup each |
| 2 quarts cold water | Turnip |
| 1 can tomatoes | Onion } cut in small pieces |
| 1 teaspoon peppercorns | Celery |
| 1 tablespoon salt | 1 sprig parsley |
| | ½ bay leaf |

1 tablespoon lean raw ham, finely chopped

Wipe meat and cut in inch cubes. Put one-half in kettle with marrow-bone, water, and tomatoes. Brown remaining half in hot frying-pan with some marrow from bone, then turn into kettle. Heat slowly to boiling-point, and cook at temperature just below boiling-point five hours.

Cook ham and vegetables with butter five minutes, then add to soup, with peppercorns, salt, parsley, and bay leaf. Cook one and one-half hours, strain, cool quickly, remove fat, and clear. Chill in ice-box and serve in bouillon cups.

### SALMON BALLS

| | |
|---|---|
| ½ tablespoon chopped onion | ¼ teaspoon paprika |
| 2 tablespoons chopped pepper | ½ cup milk |
| 3 tablespoons butter | ½ cup thin cream |
| ¼ cup flour | 1¾ cups flaked salmon |
| ¾ teaspoon salt | |

## Fourth of July Spreads

Cook onion and pepper in butter five minutes, stirring constantly. Add flour, salt, paprika, and stir until well blended; then pour on gradually, while stirring constantly, milk and cream. Bring to the boiling-point and add salmon. Spread on a plate to cool. Shape in the form of balls, dip in crumbs, egg and crumbs, fry in deep fat, and drain on brown paper. Serve piled in fours around a mound of creamed peas. Put a small American flag in balls that are on top of groups.

### SWEETBREAD SALAD

Parboil a pair of sweetbreads twenty minutes; drain, cool, and cut in one-half-inch cubes. Mix with an equal quantity of cucumber cut in one-half-inch dice. Season with salt, pepper, and paprika, and moisten with dressing. Arrange in nests of lettuce leaves.

For the dressing, beat one-half cup heavy cream until stiff, using Dover egg-beater. Add three tablespoons vinegar very slowly, continuing the beating, then season highly with salt, pepper, and paprika.

### LENOX SANDWICHES

Blanch and shred two ounces almonds. Cook in enough butter to prevent burning until deli-

110    Fourth of July Spreads

cately browned. Mix two tablespoons chopped pickles, one tablespoon Worcestershire Sauce, one tablespoon chutney, one-fourth teaspoon salt, and a few grains cayenne. Pour over almonds and cook two minutes, stirring constantly. Mash a cream cheese and season with salt and paprika. Spread unsweetened wafer crackers with cheese mixture, sprinkle with nuts, and put together in pairs. Pile on a plate covered with a doiley. White bread may be used in place of wafers.

### STRAWBERRY BISCUIT MACAROON

Fill a brick mold to one-half its depth with strawberry juice, diluted with one-third the quantity of water; then sweeten to taste. Fill mold to overflow with Macaroon Cream, adjust cover, pack in salt and ice, using equal parts, and let stand three hours.

### MACAROON CREAM

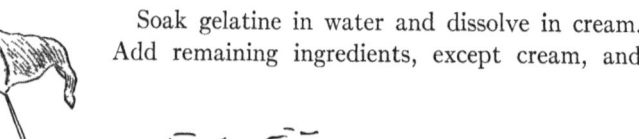

½ tablespoon granulated gelatine
3 tablespoons cold water
¼ cup scalded cream
½ tablespoon vanilla
⅔ cup rolled macaroons
Few grains salt
1 pint thin cream
¼ cup powdered sugar

Soak gelatine in water and dissolve in cream. Add remaining ingredients, except cream, and

Fourth of July Spreads

when mixture begins to thicken, fold in the whip from cream.

### COCOANUT RINGS

½ cup butter  2 teaspoons baking powder
1 cup sugar  White 1 egg
1 egg  1 tablespoon sugar
1¾ cups flour  Shredded cocoanut

Cream the butter, add sugar gradually, and egg well beaten, then add flour mixed and sifted with baking powder. Chill, toss one-half mixture on a floured board, and roll one-eighth inch thick. Shape with a doughnut cutter. Brush over with white of egg and sprinkle with sugar and cocoanut. Place on a buttered sheet and bake eight minutes in a slow oven.

### LADY BALTIMORE CAKE

1 cup butter  3½ cups flour
2 cups sugar  2 teaspoons baking powder
1 cup milk  1 teaspoon vanilla
  Whites 6 eggs

Cream butter and add gradually, while beating constantly, sugar. Mix and sift flour and baking powder, and add alternately with milk to first mixture; then add flavoring and cut and fold in whites of eggs, beaten until stiff and dry. Bake in three buttered and floured tins, seven

## Fourth of July Spreads

inches square. Put layers together with **Fruit and Nut Filling**, and cover with Fruit and Nut Filling and Ice Cream Frosting.

### FRUIT AND NUT FILLING

3 cups sugar    1 cup chopped raisins
1 cup water    1 cup chopped pecan nut
Whites 3 eggs      meats
5 figs, cut in thin strips

Cook sugar and water in a smooth graniteware saucepan until syrup will spin a thread when dropped from tip of spoon. Pour gradually, while beating constantly, on to the whites of eggs beaten until stiff, and continue the beating until of right consistency to spread, then add remaining ingredients. One-half this quantity may be made and used between layers only.

### ICE CREAM FROSTING

2 cups sugar    Whites 2 eggs
⅓ cup water    ½ teaspoon vanilla

Cook sugar and water in a smooth graniteware saucepan until syrup will spin a thread when dropped from tip of spoon. Pour gradually while beating constantly on to the whites of eggs beaten until stiff (but not dry), and continue the beating until of right consistency to spread, then add flavoring.

Fourth of July Spreads

## FOURTH OF JULY PUNCH

1 cup sugar
½ cup water
1 can sliced pineapple, cut in pieces
Juice 2 lemons
Juice 2 oranges
½ cup raspberry syrup
¼ cup brandy
1 pint bottle Moselle wine
1 pint bottle Apollinaris

Boil sugar and water five minutes and add remaining ingredients. Pour over a cake of ice.

# Fourth of July Spreads

## MENU No. II

*"Ah! what noise is that? Your pardon, madam; only a harmless entertainment after my own country fashion."*

Lucullus Lobster

Jellied Veal, Horseradish Sauce

Finger Rolls  Sembrich Sandwiches

Orange Ice Cream with Crushed Strawberries

Nut Wafers  Lemon Queens

Claret Punch

### LUCULLUS LOBSTER

Split a two-pound live lobster, remove claws, and crack. Cook one-half tablespoon finely chopped shallot and one and one-half tablespoons finely chopped carrot in one tablespoon butter five minutes. Add one sprig thyme, bit of bay leaf, one-half teaspoon salt, three-fourths cup brown stock, and one-half cup canned tomatoes. Add lobster, cover, and cook twenty minutes. Remove meat from lobster and cut in small pieces. Strain liquor in pan; there should be one cup. Thicken liquor with two tablespoons butter and three tablespoons flour, cooked together. Add lobster meat to sauce with one and one-half tablespoons sherry wine. Fill buttered ramequin dishes with mixture, cover with buttered crumbs, and bake until crumbs are browned.

### JELLIED VEAL

Soak one tablespoon granulated gelatine in one-fourth cup cold water, and dissolve in one cup boiling water; then add one-fourth cup each sugar and vinegar, two tablespoons lemon juice, and one teaspoon salt. Strain, cool, and when beginning to stiffen add one and one-half cups cold cooked veal cut in small cubes and one and one-half canned pimientos cut in small pieces.

# Fourth of July Spreads

Turn into a mold and chill. Remove from mold, cut in thin slices, and serve with

## HORSERADISH SAUCE

Mix one tablespoon tarragon vinegar, two tablespoons grated horseradish root, one teaspoon English mustard, one-half teaspoon salt, and a few grains cayenne, then add one-half cup heavy cream, beaten until stiff, and three tablespoons mayonnaise dressing. Evaporated horseradish may be used.

## FINGER ROLLS

½ cup heavy cream  1 yeast cake
1 tablespoon sugar  ¼ cup lukewarm water
¼ tablespoon salt  1½ cups flour

Scald cream and add sugar and salt. When mixture is lukewarm, add yeast cake dissolved in lukewarm water and flour. Toss on a slightly floured board and knead. Cover and let rise, cut down, toss on a floured board, and pat and roll to one-fourth inch in thickness. Shape with a lady-finger cutter, first dipped in flour, place in a buttered pan, again let rise, and bake in a moderate oven. Brush over with melted butter and return to oven to glaze.

### SEMBRICH SANDWICHES

Cut white bread in one-fourth-inch slices and spread four slices on both sides sparingly with butter, which has been worked until creamy; remaining two slices on but one side. Put between slices finely chopped cold boiled ham moistened with cream and seasoned with mustard and cayenne, and chopped nut meats moistened with mayonnaise dressing; there should be three layers of each, alternating mixtures. Repeat until a sufficient quantity is prepared Fold in cheese-cloth, press under a weight, and keep in a cool place until serving time. Cut in one-fourth-inch slices for serving.

### ORANGE ICE CREAM WITH CRUSHED STRAWBERRIES

| | |
|---|---|
| 1 cup heavy cream | 2 cups orange juice |
| 1 cup thin cream | Sugar |

Add cream slowly to orange juice, sweeten to taste, freeze, and mold. Remove from mold to chilled serving dish and surround with fresh strawberries, mashed and sweetened. Garnish with selected berries.

## Fourth of July Spreads

### NUT WAFERS

½ cup butter
1 egg
¼ cup pecan nut meats
½ cup sugar
½ tablespoon cinnamon
¼ tablespoon cloves
¼ tablespoon nutmeg
Grated rind ½ lemon
2 tablespoons brandy
2 cups flour

Cream the butter, and add egg well beaten and nuts finely chopped; then add sugar gradually while beating constantly. Add brandy, lemon rind, and flour mixed and sifted with spices. Toss on a floured board, roll to one-fourth inch in thickness, shape with a small cutter first dipped in flour, and bake on a buttered sheet in a slow oven until delicately browned.

### LEMON QUEENS

¼ lb. butter
½ lb sugar
Grated rind 1 lemon
¾ tablespoon lemon juice
Yolks 4 eggs
5 ozs flour
¼ teaspoon salt
¼ teaspoon soda (scant)
Whites 4 eggs

Cream the butter, add sugar gradually, and continue beating. Then add grated rind, lemon juice, and yolks of eggs beaten until thick and lemon colored. Mix and sift soda, salt, and flour, add to first mixture, and beat thoroughly. Add whites of eggs beaten stiff. Bake from twenty to twenty-five minutes in small tins.

## Fourth of July Spreads

### CLARET PUNCH

| | |
|---|---|
| 1 quart cold water | Few shavings lemon rind |
| ½ cup raisins | 1⅓ cups orange juice |
| 2 cups sugar | ⅓ cup lemon juice |
| 1 pint claret wine | |

Put raisins in cold water, bring slowly to boiling-point, and boil twenty minutes; strain, add sugar and lemon rind, and boil five minutes. Add fruit juice, cool, strain, pour in claret, and dilute with ice-water.

## Fourth of July Spreads

### MENU No. III

*"I feel the old convivial glow (unaided)
o'er me stealing,—
The warm, champagny, old particular
brandy punchy feeling."*
                                        O. W. Holmes.

Molded Sweetbreads Truffle Sauce

Tyrolienne Halibut

Sweedish Rings      Graham Sandwiches

Strawberry Ice Cream     Neuremburghs

Fruit Punch

## MOLDED SWEETBREADS

Parboil a pair of sweetbreads and cut in small cubes. Fold into a chicken forcemeat and turn into a mold, first garnished with slices of truffles cut in fancy shapes. Set in pan of hot water, cover with buttered paper, and bake until firm. Remove from mold and pour around Truffle Sauce.

## CHICKEN FORCEMEAT

Finely chop the breast of an uncooked chicken, pound in a mortar, then rub through a sieve. Add gradually the whites of two eggs and work until smooth. Season highly with salt and paprika, and add heavy cream until of right consistency, which can only be determined by cooking a small ball in boiling salted water. When mixture will not keep in shape, more white of egg is needed. If too stiff, add more cream.

## TRUFFLE SAUCE

Melt three tablespoons butter, add four tablespoons flour, and pour on gradually, while stirring constantly, three-fourths cup each cream and chicken stock. Bring to the boiling point, season with salt and paprika, and add two tablespoons chopped truffles.

## Fourth of July Spreads

### TYROLIENNE HALIBUT

Wipe two and one-half pounds halibut, tie in cheese-cloth, and cook in Court Bouillon until fish leaves bones. Chill, separate into flakes, season with salt, and mold in a salad bowl. Cover with Tyrolienne Sauce and garnish with thin slices of lemon, capers, and gherkins cut to represent fans.

### COURT BOUILLON

⅓ cup each carrot, onion, and celery, cut in small pieces
2 sprigs parsley
2 tablespoons butter
6 peppercorns
2 cloves
½ bay leaf
1 tablespoon salt
2 tablespoons vinegar
2 quarts water

Cook carrot, onion, celery, and parsley with butter three minutes; add remaining ingredients and bring to the boiling-point.

### SAUCE TYROLIENNE

To three-fourths cup mayonnaise add one-half tablespoon each finely chopped capers and parsley, one finely chopped gherkin, and one-half can tomatoes, stewed, strained, and cooked until reduced to two tablespoons.

## Fourth of July Spreads

### SWEEDISH RINGS

Work into one cup bread dough one-half cup butter and one-fourth cup lard. When thoroughly blended, toss on a floured board and knead, using enough flour to prevent dough from sticking. Cut off small pieces and roll, using both hands, until four and one-half inches long and one-third inch in diameter; then shape into rings. Sprinkle with chopped almonds seasoned with salt, arrange on a buttered sheet, and bake in a hot oven.

### GRAHAM SANDWICHES

Cut Graham bread in one-fourth-inch slices and spread with cream cheese mashed and moistened with French dressing. Sprinkle one-half the pieces with chopped walnut meats and cover with remaining pieces. Remove crusts and cut slices in halves diagonally, making triangles. Arrange on a plate covered with a doiley.

### STRAWBERRY ICE CREAM

3 pints thin cream     2 cups sugar
2 boxes berries     Few grains salt

Wash and hull berries, sprinkle with sugar, cover, and let stand two hours. Mash and squeeze through cheese-cloth then add cream and salt. Freeze, using three parts finely crushed ice

# Fourth of July Spreads

to one part rock salt, and mold. Remove from mold to chilled serving dish and garnish with one cup selected strawberries.

## NEUREMBURGHS

2 eggs
½ cup powdered sugar
¾ cup flour
⅓ teaspoon salt
⅓ teaspoon cinnamon
⅓ teaspoon cloves
1 tablespoon orange peel, finely cut
Grated rind ½ lemon
¾ cup Jordan almonds

Beat the whites of the eggs until stiff, and add sugar gradually, continuing the beating. Then add yolks of eggs well beaten, flour mixed and sifted with salt and spices, orange peel, and lemon rind. Blanch almonds, cut in small pieces crosswise, and bake in a slow oven until well browned. Fold into the mixture, and drop by spoonfuls on a sheet dredged with cornstarch and powdered sugar in equal proportions. Bake in a moderate oven.

## FRUIT PUNCH

1 quart cold water
2 cups sugar
2 cups chopped pineapple
1 cup orange-juice
½ cup lemon juice
½ cup raspberry syrup

Boil water, sugar, and pineapple twenty minutes; add fruit juice, cool, strain, and dilute with ice-water.

# HALLOWE'EN SPREADS

# Hallowe'en Spreads

## MENU NO. I.

*" This night I hold an old accustom'd feast "*

Ganser Salad        Brown Bread Sandwiches

Raised Loaf Cake    Priscilla Popped Corn

Hot Coffee

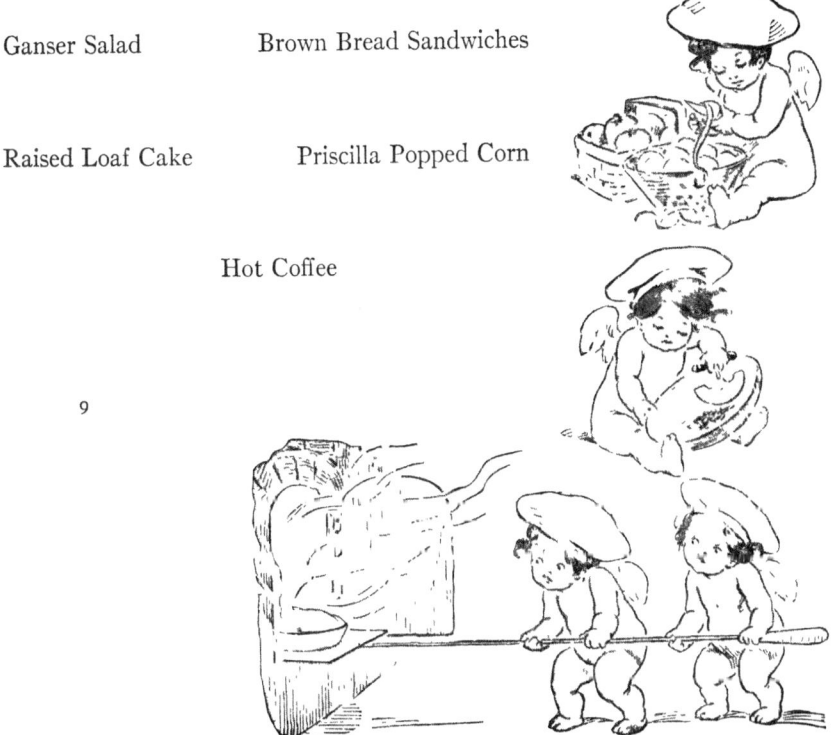

## GANSER SALAD

Soak salt herring in lukewarm water to cover, drain, and cook in boiling water fifteen minutes. Cool and separate into flakes. Add an equal quantity of small cold boiled potato cubes and one-fourth the quantity of chopped hard-boiled eggs. Marinate with a French dressing, cover, and let stand in a cold place until serving time. Beat one-fourth cup heavy cream until stiff and add two tablespoons canned pimiento purée. Mix with an equal quantity of mayonnaise dressing. Moisten mixture with dressing. Mound on a salad plate surrounded by a border of crisp lettuce leaves.

Pimiento purée is obtained by forcing canned pimientos through a purée strainer.

## BROWN BREAD SANDWICHES

Cut brown bread in thin slices, spread with creamed butter, and sprinkle with chopped peanuts, seasoned with salt. Put together in pairs and arrange in a circle overlapping one another on a plate covered with a doiley.

## Hallowe'en Spreads

### BROWN BREAD

1 cup rye meal  
1 cup granulated cornmeal  
1 cup Graham flour  
¾ tablespoon soda  
1 teaspoon salt  
¾ cup molasses  
2 cups sour milk, or 1¾ cups sweet milk or water

Mix and sift dry ingredients, add molasses and milk, stir until well mixed, turn into well-buttered one-pound baking powder boxes, and steam two hours. The covers should be buttered before being placed on boxes, and then tied down with string, otherwise the bread in rising might force off covers. Molds should never be filled more than two-thirds full.

### RAISED FRUIT LOAF

1 cup butter  
2 cups brown sugar  
2 eggs  
2 cups bread sponge  
2 teaspoons cinnamon  
1 teaspoon clove  
2 teaspoons soda  
1 teaspoon salt  
2 cups raisins  
1 cup flour

Cream butter and add gradually, while beating constantly, sugar, then add eggs well beaten, bread sponge, spices, soda and salt mixed and sifted, and raisins seeded, cut in quarters, and dredged with flour. Turn into two buttered and floured oblong pans. Let rise two and one-half

hours and bake in a moderate oven sixty minutes. Cover with Portsmouth Frosting.

For the bread sponge mix one tablespoon each butter, sugar, and salt, add one yeast cake dissolved in one cup lukewarm water, and two and one-half cups flour. Let rise until mixture is light.

### PORTSMOUTH FROSTING

2 tablespoons cream  2 teaspoons melted butter
Confectioners' sugar  ½ teaspoon vanilla

Add confectioners' sugar to cream until mixture is of right consistency to spread, then add butter and vanilla and beat two minutes.

### PRISCILLA POPPED CORN

2 quarts popped corn  2 cups brown sugar
2 tablespoons butter  ½ cup water
½ teaspoon salt

Put butter in saucepan, and when melted add sugar, salt, and water. Bring to boiling-point and let boil sixteen minutes. Pour over corn, and stir until every kernel is well coated with mixture.

### COFFEE

1 cup coffee  1 cup cold water
1 egg  6 cups boiling water

## Hallowe'en Spreads

Scald coffee-pot. Wash egg, break, and beat slightly. Dilute with one-half the cold water, add crushed shell, and mix with coffee. Turn into coffee-pot, pour on boiling water, and stir thoroughly. Place on front of range, and boil three minutes. If not boiled, coffee is cloudy; if boiled too long, too much tannic acid is developed. The spout of pot should be covered or stuffed with soft paper to prevent escape of fragrant aroma. Stir and pour some in a cup to be sure that spout is free from grounds. Return to coffee-pot and repeat. Add remaining cold water, which perfects clearing. Cold water, being heavier than hot water, sinks to the bottom, carrying grounds with it. Place on back of range for ten minutes, where coffee will not boil. Serve at once with cut sugar and cream.

# Hallowe'en Spreads

## MENU NO. II.

*"When the apples are all gathered
And the chestnut trees are bare,
When there's frost upon the garden
And a chillness in the air,
While a breath of early winter
Finds the meadows brown and sere,
Comes the welcome time for keeping
Glad the Halloween cheer."*

Rob's Rarebit        Zephyrettes

      Sultana Fudge

      German Punch

136  Hallowe'en Spreads

### ROB'S RAREBIT

| | |
|---|---|
| 2 tablespoons butter | 1/3 teaspoon soda |
| 2 tablespoons flour | 2 cups finely cut cheese |
| 3/4 cup thin cream | 2 eggs, slightly beaten |
| 3/4 cup stewed and strained tomatoes | Salt |
| | Mustard |

Cayenne

Put butter in chafing-dish, when melted, add flour. Pour on, gradually, cream, and as soon as mixture thickens add tomatoes mixed with soda; then add cheese, eggs, and seasonings to taste. Serve, as soon as cheese has melted, on toasted bread or unsweetened wafer crackers.

### SULTANA FUDGE

| | |
|---|---|
| 2 cups sugar | 2 squares chocolate |
| 1/2 cup milk | 1 teaspoon vanilla |
| 1/4 cup molasses | 1/4 cup English walnut |
| 1/4 cup butter | meat, cut in pieces |
| 1/4 cup Sultana raisins | |

Put butter into a saucepan, when melted, add sugar, milk, and molasses. Heat to boiling-point and boil seven minutes. Add chocolate and stir until chocolate is melted, then boil seven minutes longer. Remove from fire, beat until creamy, add nuts, raisins, and vanilla, and pour at once into a buttered tin. Cool slightly and mark in squares.

## Hallowe'en Spreads

### GERMAN PUNCH

1 cup grape juice
1 cup sweet cider
½ cup grapefruit juice
Juice of 1 lemon
2 pint bottles mineral water
Sugar

Mix first five ingredients and add sugar to taste. Pour into punch bowl over a large cake of ice. Many think a few gratings of nutmeg an improvement to this punch. Serve in punch glasses.

# Hallowe'en Spreads

## MENU NO. III.

*"Sirs, you are very welcome to our house
It must appear in other ways than words.
Therefore, I scant this breathing courtesy."*

Hamlin Ham Timbales        Ribbon Sandwiches

Nut Ginger Cookies                Peneuche

Cider

## Hallowe'en Spreads

### HAMLIN HAM TIMBALES

½ tablespoon granulated gelatine
1½ tablespoons cold water
¾ cup chicken stock
½ cup chopped cooked ham
½ cup chopped cooked chicken
½ pint heavy cream
⅛ teaspoon paprika
Few grains cayenne

Soak gelatine in water and dissolve in stock. Add chopped meat and stir until mixture begins to thicken; then add cream, beaten until stiff, and seasonings. Mold, chill, and serve on lettuce leaves. Garnish with mayonnaise dressing.

### RIBBON SANDWICHES

Cut white and Graham bread in one-fourth inch slices, having four slices of white and three of Graham. Spread two slices of white bread and Graham bread on both sides with creamed butter, spread remaining two pieces of white bread on but one side. Beginning with a white slice (buttered on but one side) pile in seven layers, alternating bread, and have second slice of white bread (unbuttered on one side) on top. Wrap in cheese-cloth and press under a light weight. Cut in one-fourth inch slices (for serving); then cut in halves crosswise.

## Hallowe'en Spreads

### NUT GINGER COOKIES

1 cup molasses  1/2 cup shortening, melted
1 3/4 teaspoons soda  2 teaspoons ginger
1 cup sour milk  1 teaspoon salt
Flour  Nut meats

Add soda to molasses and beat thoroughly; add milk, shortening, ginger, salt, and flour. Enough flour must be used to make mixture of right consistency to drop easily from spoon. Let stand several hours in a cold place to thoroughly chill. Toss one-half mixture at a time on slightly floured board and roll lightly to one-fourth inch in thickness. Shape with a round cutter two inches in diameter, first dipped in flour, and place a half nut meat (preferably English walnuts) in centre of each. Bake on a buttered sheet.

### PENEUCHE

1 tablespoon butter  1/3 cup milk
2 cups brown sugar  3/4 cup chopped peanuts
1/4 teaspoon salt

Put butter in saucepan, and when melted add sugar and milk. Bring to the boiling-point and let boil twelve minutes. Remove from range, add nuts sprinkled with salt, and beat until creamy. Turn into a buttered tin. Cool slightly and mark in squares.

A THANKSGIVING DINNER TABLE.

THANKSGIVING DINNERS

## Thanksgiving Dinners

### MENU NO. I.

*" Thrice happy time,
Best portion of the various year, in which
Nature rejoiceth, smiling on her works
Lovely, to full perfection wrought."*

Oysters with Sherry

Thanksgiving Soup       Popped Corn

Roast Stuffed Turkey       Brown Gravy

Sweet Potatoes à la Bement       Boiled Onions

Turnip Croquettes       Cranberry Conserve

Chicken Pie

Chiffonade Dressed Lettuce

Puritan Pudding       Foamy Brandy Sauce

Mince Pie       Pumpkin Pie

Nuts and Raisins       Assorted Fruit

Café Noir

## OYSTERS WITH SHERRY

Allow six small oysters for each person and pour over two tablespoons sherry wine, mixed with a few grains each of salt and cayenne. Let stand in ice-box for fifteen minutes. Serve in cocktail glasses.

## THANKSGIVING SOUP

| | |
|---|---|
| 1 can corn | ½ can tomatoes |
| 1 quart milk | ¼ teaspoon soda |
| 2 slices onion | ⅓ cup butter |
| 3 tablespoons flour | 2 teaspoons salt |
| ½ cup water | ⅛ teaspoon pepper |

Scald milk with corn and onion. Mix flour with water to form a smooth paste and add scalded milk. Cook twenty minutes, stirring constantly until mixture thickens, rub through a sieve. Cook tomatoes ten minutes, add soda, and rub through a sieve. Combine mixtures, add butter bit by bit, and seasonings. Accompany with popped corn

## ROAST TURKEY

Dress, clean, stuff, and truss a ten-pound cock turkey. Place on its side on rack in a dripping-pan, rub entire surface with salt, and spread breast, legs, and wings with one-third cup butter,

# Thanksgiving Dinners

rubbed until creamy and mixed with one-fourth cup flour. Dredge bottom of pan with flour. Place in a hot oven, and when flour on turkey begins to brown, reduce heat, baste with fat in pan, and add two cups boiling water. Continue basting every fifteen minutes until turkey is cooked, which will require about three hours. For basting, use one-half cup butter melted in one-half cup boiling water, and after this is used baste with fat in pan. During cooking turn turkey frequently, that it may brown evenly. If turkey is browning too fast, cover with buttered paper to prevent burning. Remove string and skewers, place bird on hot platter, and garnish with sliced canned pineapple (drained, dried on a towel, and sautéd in butter), small molds of cranberry conserve placed on pineapple, and celery tips.

## STUFFING

| | |
|---|---|
| 2 cups cracker crumbs | Salt |
| ½ cup melted butter | Pepper |
| Sage | ⅔ cup scalded milk |
| 1 egg | ⅔ cup hot water |

Melt butter in milk and water, and pour over crackers, to which seasonings have been added, then add egg slightly beaten.

## BROWN GRAVY

Pour off liquid in pan in which turkey has been roasted. From liquid skim off six tablespoons fat; return fat to pan and brown with six tablespoons flour, pour on gradually three cups stock in which giblets, neck, and tips of wings have been cooked, or use liquor left in pan. Cook five minutes, season with salt and pepper, strain.

## SWEET POTATOES À LA BEMENT

Pare sweet potatoes and cut in one-third-inch slices lengthwise. Parboil ten minutes in boiling salted water to cover, drain, and sauté in butter. Remove to a hot serving dish, pour over Jamaica rum, and light when sending to table.

## BOILED ONIONS

Put onions in cold water and remove skins while under water. Drain, put in a saucepan, and cover with boiling salted water; boil five minutes, drain, and again cover with boiling salted water. Cook one hour or until soft, but not broken. Drain, add a small quantity of milk, cook five minutes, and season with butter, salt, and pepper.

Thanksgiving Dinners

### TURNIP CROQUETTES

Wash, pare, and cut turnips in quarters Steam until tender, mash, pressing out all water that is possible. This is best accomplished by wringing in cheese-cloth. Season one and one-fourth cups with salt and pepper, then add yolks of two eggs slightly beaten. Cool, shape in small croquettes, dip in crumbs, egg and crumbs again, fry in deep fat, and drain.

### CRANBERRY CONSERVE

1 quart cranberries
1⅓ cups water
¼ lb. seeded raisins
½ lb. walnut meats
1 orange
1½ lbs. sugar

Pick over and wash cranberries, put in a stewpan with one-half the water and boil until skins break. Force through a strainer and add remaining water, raisins, nut meats broken in pieces, orange finely cut (seeds being removed), and sugar. Bring to the boiling-point and let boil twenty-five minutes. Mold and chill.

### PUFF PASTE

1 pound butter          1 pound pastry flour
            Cold water

Wash the butter, pat and fold until no water flies. Reserve two tablespoons of butter, and

shape remainder into a circular piece one-half inch thick, and put on floured board. Work two tablespoons of butter into flour with the tips of fingers of the right hand. Moisten to a dough with cold water, turn on slightly floured board, and knead one minute. Cover with towel and let stand five minutes.

Pat and roll one-fourth inch thick, keeping paste a little wider than long, and corners square. If this cannot be accomplished with rolling-pin, draw into shape with fingers. Place butter on centre of lower half of paste. Cover butter by folding upper half of paste over it. Press edges firmly, to enclose as much air as possible.

Fold right side of paste over enclosed butter, the left side under enclosed butter. Turn paste half-way round, cover, and let stand five minutes. Pat, and roll one-fourth inch thick, having paste longer than wide, lifting often to prevent paste from sticking, and dredging board slightly with flour when necessary. Fold from ends toward centre, making three layers. Cover, and let stand five minutes. Repeat twice, turning paste half-way round each time before rolling. After fourth rolling, fold from ends to centre, and double, making four layers. Put in cold place to chill;

## Thanksgiving Dinners

if outside temperature is not sufficiently cold, fold paste in a towel, put in a dripping-pan, and place between dripping-pans of crushed ice. If paste is to be kept for several days, wrap in a napkin, put in tin pail and cover tightly, then put in cold place; if in ice-box, do not allow pail to come in direct contact with ice.

Baking of puff paste requires as much care and judgment as making. After shaping, chill thoroughly before baking. Puff paste requires hot oven, greatest heat coming from the bottom, that the paste may properly rise. While rising it is often necessary to decrease the heat by lifting covers or opening the check to stove. Turn frequently that it may rise evenly.

*Rules for Washing Butter.*—Scald and chill an earthen bowl. Heat palms of hands in hot water and chill in cold water. By following these directions, butter will not adhere to bowl nor hands. Wash butter in bowl by squeezing with hands until soft and waxy, placing bowl under a cold-water faucet and allowing water to run. A small amount of butter may be washed by using a wooden spoon in place of the hands.

## CHICKEN PIE

Dress, clean, and cut up two young fowls or chickens. Put in a stewpan with one-half onion, sprig of parsley, and bit of bay leaf; cover with boiling water, and cook slowly until tender. When chicken is half cooked, add one-half tablespoon salt and one-eighth teaspoon pepper. Remove chicken, strain stock, skim off fat, and then cook until reduced to four cups. Thicken stock with one-third cup flour diluted with enough cold water to pour easily. Place a small cup in centre of baking-dish, arrange around it pieces of chicken, removing some of the larger bones, pour over gravy, and cool. Cover with pie-crust in which several incisions have been made, that there may be an outlet for escape of steam and gases. Wet edge of crust and put around a rim, having rim come close to edge. Bake in a moderate oven until crust is well risen and browned. Roll remnants of pastry and cut in diamond-shaped pieces, bake, and serve with pie when reheated. If puff paste is used, it is best to bake top separately.

## Thanksgiving Dinners

### CHIFFONADE DRESSED LETTUCE

Remove leaves from stalks of one head lettuce, discarding outside wilted ones. Wash in very cold water, drain, and dry on a towel. Arrange in as nearly the original shape as possible and serve with

### CHIFFONADE DRESSING

2 tablespoons parsley  
2 tablespoons red pepper  
1 teaspoon shallot  
2 hard-boiled eggs  
   each, finely chopped  
½ teaspoon black pepper  
¼ teaspoon paprika  
1 teaspoon salt  
6 tablespoons olive oil  
2 tablespoons vinegar

Mix ingredients, chill thoroughly, and shake two minutes.

### PURITAN PUDDING

9 common crackers  
Butter  
1¼ cups seeded raisins  
3 pints milk  
6 eggs, well beaten  
¾ cup sugar  
1 teaspoon salt  
1½ teaspoons vanilla  
½ grated nutmeg  
2 cups cream

Split crackers and butter generously. Cover bottom of buttered pudding dish with crackers and sprinkle with one-third the raisins. Repeat twice. Mix remaining ingredients, excepting cream, and pour over crackers. Let stand three

hours, then add cream.  Cover, and cook in a very slow oven four hours.  Serve with

### FOAMY BRANDY SAUCE

| ¼ cup butter | Yolks 2 eggs |
| 1 cup brown sugar | ½ cup cream |
| 2 tablespoons brandy | Whites 2 eggs |

Cream butter and add gradually, while beating constantly, sugar, then add brandy (very slowly), yolks of eggs beaten until thick, and cream.  Cook in double boiler, stirring constantly until mixture thickens, then pour gradually on to the stiffly beaten whites of eggs.

### QUALITY PASTE

| ¼ cup lard | ½ cup butter |
| 2 cups pastry flour | Cold water |

Chop lard into flour (once sifted) and moisten to a very stiff dough with water, using a case-knife.  Cut into dough butter, and chill for three hours.  Toss on a floured board, dredged sparingly with flour, and pat with rolling-pin and then roll to one-fourth inch thick, keeping paste longer than wide and corners square.  If this cannot be accomplished with the rolling-pin, draw into shape with the fingers.  Fold so as to make three layers, turn half-way round, pat, and roll out; repeat three times, when paste is ready to use.

## MINCE PIE MEAT

4 lbs lean beef
2 lbs. beef suet
Baldwin apples
3 lbs. sugar
2 cups molasses
2 quarts cider
4 lbs. raisins, seeded and cut in pieces
3 lbs. currants
½ lb finely cut citron
1 quart cooking brandy
1 tablespoon cinnamon and mace
1 tablespoon powdered cloves
2 grated nutmegs
1 teaspoon pepper
Salt to taste

Cover meat and suet with boiling water and cook until tender, then cool in water in which they are cooked, the suet will rise to top, forming a cake of fat, which may be easily removed. Finely chop meat, and add it to twice the amount of finely chopped apples. The apples should be quartered, cored, and pared previous to chopping, or skins may be left on, which is not an objection if apples are finely chopped. Add sugar, molasses, cider, raisins, currants, and citron; also suet and stock in which meat and suet were cooked, reduced to one and one-half cups. Heat gradually, stir occasionally, and cook slowly two hours; then add brandy and spices.

## Thanksgiving Dinners

### MINCE PIE

Line a perforated tin pie plate with Quality Paste, and fill with mince meat. Wet edges of under crust with cold water, cover with upper crust, and press edges together. Ornament with a rim and perforate upper crust that steam may escape.

### PUMPKIN PIE

1½ cups steamed and strained pumpkin
⅔ cup brown sugar
1 teaspoon cinnamon
½ teaspoon ginger
½ teaspoon salt
2 eggs, slightly beaten
1½ cups milk
½ cup cream

Mix ingredients in order given and bake in one crust.

## Thanksgiving Dinners

### MENU NO. II.

*"How many things by season seasoned are
To their right frame and true perfection."*
                                   Shakspere.

Celery with Caviare

Oyster Soup    Olives    Oyster Crackers

Roast Turkey            Giblet Stuffing

Potato and Spinach Croquettes

Glazed Silver Skins    Squash Soufflé

Frozen Cranberries

Cucumber Cups    Brown Bread Sandwiches

New England Thanksgiving Pudding,

Mousselaine Sauce

Vanilla Ice Cream, Dewey Sauce

Pastry Jelly Rolls    Assorted Nuts    Bonbons

Toasted Crackers    Stuffed Dates

Café Noir

## CELERY WITH CAVIARE

Cut celery in two-inch pieces and curl. Spread uncurled portions with caviare. Arrange for individual service on a small crisp lettuce leaf on a fancy plate and garnish with a radish cut to represent a tulip.

*To Curl Celery.*—Cut thick stalks of celery in two-inch pieces. With a sharp knife, beginning at outside of stalks, make five cuts parallel with each other, extending one-third the length of pieces. Make six cuts at right angles to cuts already made. Cut other end in same fashion. Put pieces in cold or ice water and let stand several hours, when they will curl back, and celery will be found very crisp.

## OYSTER SOUP

| | |
|---|---|
| 1 quart oysters | 1 teaspoon Worcestershire Sauce |
| 1 quart chicken stock | ½ teaspoon salt |
| ⅓ cup butter | Few grains cayenne |
| ⅓ cup flour | 1 teaspoon finely chopped parsley |
| 1 cup cream | |

Pick over oysters and parboil in their own liquor five minutes. Strain liquor, add stock, and bring to boiling-point. Melt butter, add flour, and stir until well blended, then pour on gradually,

# Thanksgiving Dinners

while stirring constantly, the hot stock. Bring to the boiling-point and let simmer five minutes. Just before serving add cream and parboiled oysters.

## ROAST TURKEY

Dress, clean, stuff, truss, and roast a ten-pound turkey. Remove to hot platter and garnish with celery tips.

## GIBLET STUFFING

Finely chop cooked giblets. Split sixteen common crackers and spread with butter, allowing one-fourth tablespoon to each half. Pour over two and three-fourths cups stock in which giblets were cooked. When crackers have taken up stock, add chopped giblets, and season with salt and pepper.

## CHESTNUT GRAVY

Pour off liquid in pan in which turkey has been roasted. From liquid skim off six tablespoons fat; return fat to pan and brown with six tablespoons flour; pour on gradually three cups stock in which giblets, neck, and tips of wings have been cooked, or use liquor left in pan. Cook five minutes, season with salt and pepper, strain. Add one-half cup French chestnuts blanched, boiled, and cut in pieces.

### POTATO AND SPINACH CROQUETTES

To two cups hot riced potatoes add two tablespoons butter, yolks two eggs slightly beaten, and one-fourth cup finely chopped cooked spinach. Season with salt and pepper. Shape same as potato croquettes, dip in flour, egg and crumbs, fry in deep fat, and drain on brown paper. Pile on a hot serving plate and garnish with parsley.

### GLAZED SILVER SKINS

Peel twelve small onions and cook in boiling salted water until tender. Drain thoroughly and sauté in three tablespoons butter, to which is added one tablespoon sugar, until delicately browned.

### SQUASH SOUFFLÉ

To two cups hot steamed squash, forced through a sieve, add one tablespoon brown sugar, one teaspoon salt, one-eighth teaspoon pepper, one and one-half cups rich milk, and the yolks of two eggs beaten until thick and lemon colored. Cut and fold in the whites of two eggs, beaten until stiff and dry, turn into a buttered baking dish, and bake until firm.

# Thanksgiving Dinners

### FROZEN CRANBERRIES

Pick over and wash four cups cranberries. Add one and one-half cups boiling water and two and one-fourth cups sugar and let boil twelve minutes, skimming twice during the cooking. Rub through a sieve, cool, and fill to overflowing one-half pound baking powder boxes with mixture. Pack in salt and ice, using equal parts, and let stand four hours.

### CUCUMBER CUPS

Pare cucumbers; remove a thick slice from each end, and with a sharp-pointed knife make eight grooves at equal distances lengthwise of cucumber. Cut crosswise, making three or four cup-shaped pieces; then cut in thin slices crosswise, keeping in original shape. Scoop out some of the centre of each, arrange on crisp lettuce leaves for individual service, and fill with

### CREAM FRENCH DRESSING

½ teaspoon salt           2 tablespoons vinegar
⅛ teaspoon paprika     3 tablespoons olive oil
    6 tablespoons heavy cream

Mix first four ingredients until well blended, then add cream beaten until stiff.

## Thanksgiving Dinners

### BROWN BREAD SANDWICHES

See page 130, under Hallowe'en Spreads, **Menu No. I.**

### NEW ENGLAND THANKSGIVING PUDDING

| | |
|---|---|
| 4 cups scalded milk | ⅓ cup melted butter |
| 1¼ cups rolled crackers | ½ grated nutmeg |
| 1 cup molasses | ½ teaspoon cinnamon |
| 4 eggs | 1 teaspoon salt |
| 1½ cups raisins | |

Pour milk over crackers and let stand until cool, add sugar, eggs slightly beaten, nutmeg, cinnamon, salt, and butter; parboil raisins until soft by cooking in boiling water to cover, seed, and add to mixture; turn into buttered bread pan, cover, set in larger pan of hot water, and bake slowly three hours, stirring after first half-hour to prevent raisins from settling.

### MOUSSELAINE SAUCE

| | |
|---|---|
| Yolks 4 eggs | 1 cup heavy cream |
| 1 cup powdered sugar | 1 teaspoon vanilla |
| 2 tablespoons brandy | Few grains salt |

Beat yolks of eggs until light, and add gradually, while beating constantly, sugar and brandy. Place on range and cook five minutes, stirring

# Thanksgiving Dinners

constantly. Set in pan of iced or very cold water, and beat until mixture is cold; then add cream, beaten until stiff, vanilla, and salt.

### FRENCH VANILLA ICE CREAM, DEWEY SAUCE

| | |
|---|---|
| 2 eggs | 2½ cups scalded milk |
| 1 cup sugar | 2 cups heavy cream |
| ⅛ teaspoon salt | 1 tablespoon vanilla |

Beat eggs slightly and add sugar, mixed with salt. Stir constantly while adding gradually hot milk. Cook in double boiler, continuing the stirring until mixture thickens and a slight coating is formed on the spoon. Strain, cool, and add cream and vanilla. Freeze, using three parts finely crushed ice to one part rock salt, to insure a smooth, fine-grained cream. Serve in coupe glasses with Dewey sauce.

### DEWEY SAUCE

| | |
|---|---|
| 1 cup sugar | 2 egg yolks |
| ½ cup water | 1 teaspoon Orange Curaçoa |
| | 2 tablespoons Jamaica rum |

Boil sugar and water two minutes. Pour syrup slowly, while beating constantly, on to the well-beaten yolks of eggs, return to fire and cook,

stirring constantly, until mixture thickens slightly. Cool and add flavoring.

### PASTRY JELLY ROLLS

Roll paste to one-eighth inch in thickness and cut in pieces five inches by three inches. Spread with jelly that has been beaten with a silver fork until of right consistency to spread evenly. Sprinkle with chopped pecan nut meats and roll. Place on unbuttered sheet and bake in a hot oven until delicately browned.

### STUFFED DATES

Make a cut the entire length of dates and remove stones. Fill cavities with Cream Cheese, worked until smooth and seasoned highly with salt and paprika, and shape in original form. Pile in rows on a small plate covered with a doiley.

A CHRISTMAS DINNER TABLE.

# CHRISTMAS DINNERS

## Christmas Dinners

### MENU NO. I.

*"Heap on more wood, the wind is chill;
But let it whistle as it will,
We'll keep our Christmas merry still."*
                                    Scott.

Sardine Cocktail

Chicken Consommé with Oysters    Pulled Bread

Olives                    Salted Pecans

Spanish Mackerel, Jaffa      Dressed Cucumbers

Roast Goose    Potato Stuffing    Apple Baskets

Sweet Potatoes with Sherry

Cauliflower, Hongroise        Christmas Salad

Cheese Stars    Fruit Pudding    Monroe Sauce

Parfait Armour            Lady Fingers

Bonbons

Toasted Crackers            Roquefort

Café Noir

## Christmas Dinners

### SARDINE COCKTAIL

Drain one small box sardines, free from skin and bones, and separate into small pieces. Mix one-half cup tomato catsup, two teaspoons Worcestershire Sauce, one-half teaspoon Tabasco Sauce, the juice of one lemon, and salt to taste. Add sauce to sardines, chill thoroughly, and serve in scallop shells placed on shallow small plates on a bed of crushed ice.

### CHICKEN CONSOMME WITH OYSTERS

1 pint oysters  
½ cup cold water  
4 cups chicken stock  
½ teaspoon salt  
Few grains cayenne  
½ cup cream

Wash oysters and reserve soft portions. Chop tough portions, add cold water, bring to the boiling-point, and let simmer twenty-five minutes. Strain through a double thickness of cheese-cloth and add chicken stock. Season with salt and cayenne, add cream, and soft parts of oysters cooked until plump.

### PULLED BREAD

Remove crusts from a long loaf of freshly baked water bread. Pull the bread apart until the pieces are the desired size and length, which is best accomplished by using two three-tined forks. Cook in a slow oven until delicately browned and

# Christmas Dinners

thoroughly dried. A baker's French loaf may be used for pulled bread if home-made is not at hand.

## SALTED PECANS

Buy pecan nut meats by the pound. Put one-fourth cup olive oil in a small saucepan, and when heated put in nut meats and stir constantly until they are heated and crisp. Remove with a spoon or small skimmer to brown paper, taking up as little oil as possible, and sprinkle with salt; repeat until one-fourth pound is fried.

## SPANISH MACKEREL, JAFFA

Split fish, clean, cut off head and tail, and remove backbone. Place in buttered pan, and shake over (through a fine strainer) one teaspoon salt, mixed with one-half teaspoon curry powder. Work one tablespoon butter until creamy and mix with one teaspoon Anchovy Essence. Spread fish with mixture and bake twenty-five minutes, basting three times during the baking with melted butter. Mix one-fourth cup blanched and chopped almonds, one tablespoon capers, and one-half cup brown or chicken stock, and let simmer five minutes. Pour over fish, sprinkle with buttered bread crumbs, and bake until crumbs are brown.

### ROAST GOOSE, POTATO STUFFING

Singe, remove pinfeathers, wash and scrub a goose in hot soapsuds, then draw (which is removing inside contents). Wash in cold water and wipe. Stuff, truss, sprinkle with salt and pepper, and lay six thin strips fat salt pork over breast. Place on rack in dripping-pan, put in hot oven, and bake two hours. Baste every fifteen minutes with fat in pan. Remove pork last half hour of cooking. Place on platter, cut string, and remove string and skewers. Garnish with Apple Baskets and watercress.

### POTATO STUFFING

Force eight hot boiled potatoes through a potato ricer. Add one-third cup melted butter, one cup cream, three eggs well beaten, and two medium-sized onions finely chopped. Beat two minutes and season with salt and pepper.

### APPLE BASKETS

Cut two pieces from each apple, leaving what remains in shape of basket with handle, after cutting out pulp. Chop pulp; there should be two cups. Put in a stewpan and add three-fourths pound light brown sugar. juice and rind

# Christmas Dinners

of one lemon, one ounce ginger root, a few grains salt, and enough water to prevent apples from burning. Cover and cook slowly four hours, adding water as necessary.

## SWEET POTATOES WITH SHERRY

Season mashed boiled sweet potatoes with butter, salt, pepper, and sherry wine. Moisten with rich milk and beat vigorously. Pile lightly on hot vegetable dish.

## CAULIFLOWER HONGROISE

Prepare cauliflower as for boiled cauliflower, and steam until soft. Separate in pieces and pour over the following sauce:

Mix one and one-half teaspoons mustard, one and one-fourth teaspoons salt, one teaspoon powdered sugar, and one-fourth teaspoon paprika. Add yolks three eggs slightly beaten, one-fourth cup olive oil, and one-half cup vinegar. Cook over hot water until mixture thickens. Remove from range, and add two tablespoons butter cooked with one teaspoon finely chopped onion three minutes, and one teaspoon finely chopped parsley.

## Christmas Dinners

### CHRISTMAS SALAD

Pare and chill six medium-sized tomatoes. When ready to serve cut in eighths (not severing sections) and open like the petals of a flower on a nest of lettuce leaves. Mash a cream cheese, moisten with French dressing, and make into tiny balls about the size of a pea. Place eight cheese balls in centre of each tomato. Serve with

### DELMONICO DRESSING

½ teaspoon salt  
¼ teaspoon pepper  
½ tablespoon finely chopped parsley  
2 tablespoons vinegar  
4 tablespoons olive oil  
1 tablespoon finely chopped red pepper

Mix ingredients and stir until well blended.

### CHEESE STARS

Roll paste to one-fourth inch in thickness and sprinkle one-half with grated cheese seasoned with salt and cayenne. Fold, press edges firmly together, fold again, pat, and roll. Sprinkle with more cheese and proceed as before; repeat twice. Cut in three-inch squares and make diagonal cuts at corners, fold alternate corners to centres in such a way as to make stars. Bake on a tin sheet and arrange on a plate covered with a folded napkin.

## FRUIT PUDDING

| | |
|---|---|
| 1 cup beef suet | 1 cup raisins, seeded and cut in pieces |
| 2⅔ cups stale bread crumbs | |
| 1 cup grated carrots | ¾ cup currants |
| Yolks 4 eggs | ⅓ cup flour |
| 1⅓ cups browned sugar | 1½ teaspoons salt |
| Grated rind 1 lemon | 1 teaspoon cinnamon |
| 1 tablespoon vinegar | ½ teaspoon grated nutmeg |
| Whites 4 eggs | ¼ teaspoon cloves |

Work suet until creamy and add bread crumbs and carrots. Beat egg yolks until light and add gradually, while beating constantly, sugar. Combine mixtures and add lemon rind and vinegar. Mix fruit and dredge with flour mixed and sifted with salt and spices. Add to mixture, then add whites of eggs beaten until stiff. Turn into a buttered mold, garnished with thin strips of citron, cover, and steam three and one-half hours. Serve with

## MONROE SAUCE

| | |
|---|---|
| 1 cup brown sugar | 2 tablespoons butter |
| ⅓ cup hot water | ⅛ teaspoon salt |
| 2 tablespoons cornstarch | Few grains nutmeg |
| 2 tablespoons cold water | ½ teaspoon vanilla |
| 2 tablespoons sherry wine | |

Bring sugar and water to boiling-point and let simmer fifteen minutes. Add cold water to corn-

## Christmas Dinners

starch and stir until smooth. Add gradually to syrup, stir until ingredients are blended, then let simmer forty-five minutes. Add remaining ingredients and serve at once.

### PARFAIT ARMOUR

| | |
|---|---|
| 4 cups water | 2¼ cups orange juice |
| 2 cups sugar | ¼ cup lemon juice |
| Few grains salt | Grated rind 2 oranges |

Mix water and sugar, bring to the boiling-point, and let boil one minute. Add salt, fruit juices, and grated rind, cool, strain, and freeze, using three parts finely crushed ice to one part rock salt. Serve in tall coupe glasses.

Make depression in ice, extending one-third height of glass and having well three-fourths inch in diameter. Fill with one teaspoon Grenadine, one teaspoon Kirsch, and one-half teaspoon brandy, being sure to add liquors in order mentioned.

### LADY FINGERS

See page 41, under St. Valentine Spreads, Menu II.

## Christmas Dinners

### MENU NO. II.

*"At last the dishes were set on and grace was said. It was succeeded by a breathless pause as Mrs Cratchit, looking all along the carving knife, prepared to plunge it in the breast of the goose; but when she did, and when the long expected gush of stuffing issued forth, one murmur of delight arose all round the board, and even Tiny Tim, excited by the two young Cratchits, beat on the table with the handle of his knife and feebly cried, 'Hurrah" . . . Hallo! A great deal of steam! The pudding was out of the copper In half a minute Mrs. Cratchit entered—flushed, but smiling proudly—with the pudding, like a speckled cannon-ball, so hard and firm, blazing in half or half-a-quartern of ignited brandy and bedight with Christmas holly stuck into the top."*

From Dickens' Christmas Carol.

Grapefruit with Apricot Brandy
Filippini Consommé     Celery with Roquefort
Roast Duck     Grape Jelly
Potatoes in Cream     St. Denis Croquettes
Breslin Patties
Stuffed Tomato Salad     Somerset Sandwiches
English Plum Pudding     Brandy and Hot Sauce
Coupe Moquin
Water Crackers     Camembert
Bonbons
Café Noir

### GRAPEFRUIT WITH APRICOT BRANDY

Wipe grapefruit and cut in halves crosswise. With a small, sharp-pointed knife make a cut separating pulp from skin around entire circumference; then make cuts separating pulp from tough portion which divides fruit into sections. Remove tough portion in one piece, which may be accomplished by one cutting with scissors at stem or blossom end close to skin. Sprinkle fruit pulp left in grapefruit skin generously with sugar. Let stand ten minutes, and serve very cold. Place on fruit plate, add one-half tablespoon apricot brandy to each portion, and garnish with a candied cherry.

### FILIPPINI CONSOMME

| | |
|---|---|
| 2 cups consommé | 3 tablespoons sherry wine |
| 1 cup brown stock | Salt |
| 3 tablespoons pimiento purée | Cayenne |

Mix first four ingredients and season with salt and cayenne. Clear, using the white and shell of one egg. To obtain pimiento purée, force canned pimientos through a purée strainer.

# Christmas Dinners

## CONSOMMÉ

3 lbs. beef, poorer part of round
1 lb. marrow-bone
3 lbs. knuckle of veal
1 quart chicken stock
Carrot ⎫
Turnip ⎬ ⅓ cup each, cut in dice
Celery ⎭
⅓ cup sliced onion
2 tablespoons butter
1 tablespoon salt
1 teaspoon peppercorns
4 cloves
3 sprigs thyme
1 sprig marjoram
2 sprigs parsley
½ bay leaf
3 quarts cold water

Cut beef in one-and-one-half-inch cubes, and brown one-half in some of the marrow from marrow-bone; put remaining half in kettle with cold water, add veal cut in pieces, browned meat, and bones. Let stand one-half hour. Heat slowly to boiling-point and let simmer three hours, removing scum as it forms on top of kettle. Add one quart liquor in which a fowl was cooked and simmer two hours. Cook carrot, turnip, onion, and celery in butter five minutes, then add to soup, with remaining seasonings. Cook one and one-half hours, strain, cool quickly, remove fat, and clear.

To clear soup stock, remove fat and put quantity to be cleared in stewpan, allowing white and shell of one egg to each quart of stock. Beat egg slightly, break shell in small pieces, and

add to stock. Place on front of range and stir constantly until boiling-point is reached; boil two minutes. Set back where it may simmer twenty minutes; remove scum and strain through double thickness of cheese-cloth placed over a fine strainer. If stock to be cleared is not sufficiently seasoned, additional seasoning must be added as soon as stock has lost its jelly-like consistency, not after clearing is effected.

### BROWN SOUP STOCK

6 lbs shin of beef  
3 quarts cold water  
½ teaspoon peppercorns  
6 cloves  
½ bay leaf  
3 sprigs thyme  
1 sprig marjoram  
2 sprigs parsley  
Carrot ⎫  
Turnip ⎬ ½ cup each, cut  
Onion  ⎪ in dice  
Celery ⎭  
1 tablespoon salt

Wipe beef, and cut the lean meat in inch cubes. Brown one-third of meat in hot frying-pan in marrow from a marrow-bone. Put remaining two-thirds with bone and fat in soup kettle, add water, and let stand for thirty minutes. Place on back of range, add browned meat, and heat gradually to boiling-point. As scum rises it should be removed. Cover and cook slowly six hours, keeping below boiling-point during cook-

# Christmas Dinners

ing. Add vegetables and seasonings, cook one and one-half hours, strain, and cool as quickly as possible.

## CELERY WITH ROQUEFORT

Select short tender stalks of celery, leaving on leaves; wash and chill thoroughly. Work three-fourths tablespoon butter until creamy and add one and one-half tablespoons Roquefort cheese. Season with salt, pepper, and paprika, and spread on inside of celery stalks. Serve on crushed ice.

## ROAST DUCK

Dress and clean duck. Put in body three chopped apples mixed with one chopped onion. This stuffing is not to be served. Truss, place on rack in dripping-pan, sprinkle with salt and pepper, and dredge bird and bottom of pan with flour. Roast in a hot oven until tender, the time required being about one and one-fourth hours, basting every ten minutes with one-fourth cup butter melted in one-fourth cup boiling water, and after that is gone with fat in pan. Remove to hot platter and garnish with St. Denis croquettes and parsley.

### POTATOES IN CREAM

Wash potatoes, boil with their jackets on until soft, drain, and let stand several hours. Peel and cut in one-third inch cubes. Measure and put into a saucepan, adding one tablespoon butter to each cup potatoes. Sprinkle with salt and very generously with paprika. Add cream to cover and cook very slowly forty minutes.

### ST. DENIS CROQUETTES

| | |
|---|---|
| ¼ cup hominy | ¾ cup scalded milk |
| ½ cup boiling water | 2 tablespoons butter |
| ½ teaspoon salt | 3 teaspoons grated horse-radish root |

Steam hominy with water until it has absorbed water; then add salt and milk and steam until tender. Add butter and horseradish, shape, dip in crumbs, egg and crumbs, fry in deep fat, and drain on brown paper.

### BRESLIN PATTIES

Put one pint oysters in strainer, place over bowl, and pour over one-half cup cold water. Pick over oysters to see that no particle of shell adheres to tough muscles, and add to liquor which has been strained through cheese-cloth. Parboil oysters and again strain liquor. Melt three table-

# Christmas Dinners

spoons butter, add four and one-half tablespoons flour, and pour on gradually the oyster liquor and enough milk or cream to make one and one-half cups liquid. Season with salt, pepper, and celery salt. Reheat oysters in sauce and add one-half cup finely cut celery. Fill patty cases made of puff paste with mixture.

### STUFFED TOMATO SALAD

Skin six small tomatoes, cut a slice from stem end of each, and remove soft inside. Sprinkle inside with salt, invert, and let stand at least one-half hour. Mash one half cream cheese and add six chopped pimolas, one tablespoon tomato pulp, one tablespoon chopped parsley, one-fourth teaspoon dry mustard, and enough French Dressing to moisten. Fill tomatoes with mixture. Arrange in nests of lettuce leaves and serve with Mayonnaise Dressing.

### SOMERSET SANDWICHES

Mash a cream cheese and moisten with French Dressing. Spread thin slices of Graham bread with mixture and sprinkle with chopped pecan nut meats. Cover with bread, remove crusts, cut in finger-shaped pieces, and toast on both sides. Serve hot with a dinner salad.

## Christmas Dinners

### ENGLISH PLUM PUDDING

½ lb. stale bread crumbs
1 cup scalded milk
¼ lb. sugar
4 eggs
¾ lb. raisins, seeded, cut in pieces and floured
¼ lb. currants
2 oz. finely cut citron
½ lb. suet
¼ cup wine
½ grated nutmeg
¾ teaspoon cinnamon
⅓ teaspoon cloves
⅓ teaspoon mace
1½ teaspoons salt

Soak bread crumbs in milk, let stand until cool, add sugar, beaten yolks of eggs, raisins, currants, and citron; chop suet, and cream by using the hand, combine mixtures, then add wine, nutmeg, cinnamon, cloves, mace, and whites of eggs beaten stiff. Turn into buttered mold, cover, and steam six hours. Serve with Brandy and Hot Sauce.

### BRANDY SAUCE

Cream one-third cup butter and add gradually, while beating constantly, one cup brown sugar and two tablespoons brandy, drop by drop. Force through a pastry bag with rose tube, and garnish with green leaves and candied cherries.

### HOT SAUCE

Mix one-half cup sugar, one-half tablespoon cornstarch, and a few grains salt. Add gradually,

while stirring constantly, one cup boiling water, and boil five minutes. Remove from fire, add one tablespoon lemon juice and two tablespoons brandy; then color with fruit red.

### COUPE MOQUIN

| | |
|---|---|
| 4 cups water | ¼ cup lemon juice |
| 2 cups sugar | Grated rind of 2 oranges |
| 2 cups orange juice | 2 tablespoons Crême de Menthe |

Mix first five ingredients and freeze to a mush, then add Crême de Menthe and continue the freezing. When ready to serve, fill champagne or coupe glasses with ice and garnish with Bar-le-duc currants and candied orange peel. If one is not fond of Crême de Menthe, it may be omitted.

# WEDDING RECEPTIONS

Wedding Receptions

## MENU NO. I

*"Look down, you gods,
And on this couple drop a blessed crown."*
                                        Shakspere.

Chicken à la King        Lettuce Sandwiches

Salmon Mayonnaise        Reception Rolls

Strawberry Bombé         Lady Fingers

Salted Almonds

Wedding Cake in Boxes

Pineapple Punch

## CHICKEN À LA KING

2½ tablespoons chicken fat    ¼ cup cream
1½ tablespoons cornstarch    1 cup cold boiled fowl,
¾ teaspoon salt    cut in strips.
¾ cup chicken stock    ½ cup sautéd sliced
½ cup milk    mushroom caps
1 egg    ¼ cup pimiento strips
3 tablespoons butter

Melt chicken fat, add cornstarch, and stir until well blended, then add salt, and pour on gradually, while stirring constantly, stock, milk, and cream Bring to the boiling-point and add fowl (using preferably white meat), sautéd mushroom caps, pimiento strips, and egg slightly beaten; then add butter, bit by bit. Pimiento strips are cut from canned pimientos.

## LETTUCE SANDWICHES

Put fresh, crisp lettuce leaves, washed and thoroughly dried, between thin slices of buttered bread, having a teaspoon of mayonnaise on each leaf.

## SALMON MAYONNAISE

Wipe three slices fresh salmon cut two inches thick, place in a pan, and cover with cold water to which have been added two cloves, two slices

## Wedding Receptions

lemon, one small sliced onion, six slices carrot, one sprig parsley, one teaspoon salt, one-fourth teaspoon pepper, one-fourth cup vinegar, and one-fourth cup white wine. Cover closely and let stand three hours. Place on range and let simmer until fish is tender. Cool, place on serving dish, remove skin and bones, and spread evenly and smoothly with one and one-third cups Mayonnaise Dressing, to which has been added two teaspoons dissolved granulated gelatine. Garnish with truffles and peppers cut in fancy shapes and celery tips.

### RECEPTION ROLLS

| | |
|---|---|
| 2 cups scalded milk | 1½ teaspoons salt |
| ¼ cup butter | 1 yeast cake dissolved in |
| 2 tablespoons sugar | ¼ cup lukewarm water |
| | Flour |

Add butter, sugar, and salt to milk; when lukewarm, add dissolved yeast cake and three cups flour. Beat thoroughly, cover, and let rise until light. Cut down and add enough flour to knead (about two and one-half cups). Cover again, let rise, toss on slightly floured board, knead, pat, and roll to one-third inch thickness. Shape in small biscuits, place in rows on floured board, cover, and let rise fifteen min-

utes. With handle of large wooden spoon or toy rolling-pin roll through centre of each biscuit, brush edge of lower halves with melted butter, fold, press lightly, place in buttered pan, cover, let rise, and bake in a hot oven.

### STRAWBERRY BOMBÉ

| | |
|---|---|
| Strawberry ice | ¾ cup hot caramel syrup |
| ½ cup sugar | Yolks 4 eggs |
| ½ cup chopped blanched filberts | 1⅓ cups heavy cream |
| | ½ tablespoon vanilla |

Few grains salt

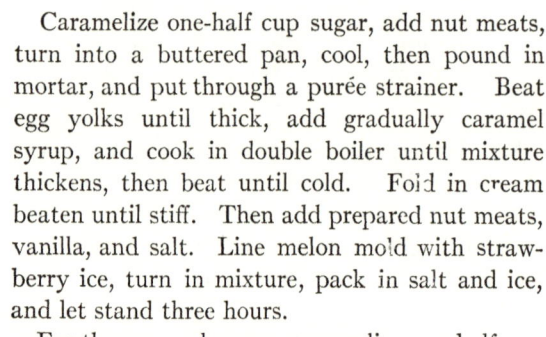

Caramelize one-half cup sugar, add nut meats, turn into a buttered pan, cool, then pound in mortar, and put through a purée strainer. Beat egg yolks until thick, add gradually caramel syrup, and cook in double boiler until mixture thickens, then beat until cold. Fold in cream beaten until stiff. Then add prepared nut meats, vanilla, and salt. Line melon mold with strawberry ice, turn in mixture, pack in salt and ice, and let stand three hours.

For the caramel syrup, caramelize one-half cup sugar, add one-half cup water, and let simmer until reduced to three-fourths cup.

# Wedding Receptions

### LADY FINGERS

See page 41, under St. Valentine Spreads, Menu No. II.

### SALTED ALMONDS

See pages 5 and 6, under New Year's Afternoon Teas, Menu No. I.

### STRAWBERRY ICE

| | |
|---|---|
| 4 cups water | 2 cups strawberry juice |
| 1½ cups sugar | 1 tablespoon lemon juice |

Mix sugar and water, add berries mashed and squeezed through double cheese-cloth, and lemon juice; strain and freeze.

### WEDDING CAKE

| | |
|---|---|
| 1 lb. butter | ¼ teaspoon soda |
| 1 lb. brown sugar | 3 lbs. raisins, seeded and cut in pieces |
| 12 eggs | 2 lbs Sultana raisins |
| 1 cup molasses | 1½ lbs citron, thinly sliced and cut in strips |
| 1 lb. flour | |
| 4 teaspoons cinnamon | |
| 4 teaspoons allspice | 1 lb currants |
| 1½ teaspoons mace | 1 cup brandy |
| 1 nutmeg grated | 4 squares chocolate, melted |

1 tablespoon hot water

## 192  Wedding Receptions

Cream the butter, add sugar gradually, and beat thoroughly. Separate yolks from whites of eggs, and beat yolks until thick and lemon colored. Add to first mixture, then add flour (excepting one-third cup, which should be reserved to dredge fruit) mixed and sifted with spices, fruit dredged with flour, brandy, chocolate, and whites of eggs beaten until stiff and dry. Just before putting into buttered bread pans add soda dissolved in hot water. Cover pans with buttered paper and steam four hours. Finish cooking by leaving in a warm oven over night.

Cover with

### ORNAMENTAL FROSTING

2 cups sugar　　　Whites 3 eggs
1 cup water　　　 ¼ teaspoon tartaric acid

Boil sugar and water until syrup, when dropped from tip of spoon, forms a long thread. Pour syrup gradually on beaten whites of eggs, beating constantly; then add acid and continue beating. When stiff enough to spread, put a thin coating over cake. Beat remaining frosting until cold and stiff enough to keep in shape after being forced through a pastry tube. After first coating on cake has hardened, cover with a thicker layer

# Wedding Receptions 193

and crease for cutting. If frosting is too stiff to spread smoothly, thin with a few drops of water. With a pastry bag and variety of tubes, cake may be ornamented as desired.

## PINEAPPLE PUNCH

| | |
|---|---|
| 2 cups water | 1 quart ice-water |
| 1¼ cups sugar | 1 can grated pineapple |
| | Juice 4 lemons |

Make a syrup by boiling water and sugar ten minutes. Add pineapple and lemon juice, cool, strain, and add ice-water. Pour over piece of ice in punch bowl, and garnish with thin slices of lemon from which the seeds have been removed.

# Wedding Receptions

## MENU NO. II

> "*Good luck
> Shall fling her old shoe after.*"
> Tennyson.

Shrimps à la Newburg

Bread and Butter Folds

Nile Salad     Salad Rolls

Manhattan Cream     Pound Cakes

Glacéd Fruits     Bride's Cake

Coffee

## Wedding Receptions

### SHRIMPS À LA NEWBURG

| | |
|---|---|
| 1 can shrimps | ½ teaspoon salt |
| 1 tablespoon sherry | Few grains cayenne |
| 1 tablespoon brandy | Slight grating nutmeg |
| ¼ cup butter | ⅓ cup thin cream |
| Yolks 2 eggs | |

Melt butter, add shrimps, which have been soaked one hour in sherry and brandy, and cook three minutes. Add seasonings, cook one minute, then add cream and yolk of eggs slightly beaten. Stir until thickened.

### BREAD AND BUTTER FOLDS

Remove end slice from bread. Spread end of loaf sparingly and evenly with butter which has been creamed. Cut off as thin as possible. Repeat until the number of slices required are prepared. Remove crusts, put together in pairs, and cut in squares, oblongs, or triangles. Use white, entire wheat, or Graham bread. Three-layer sandwiches are attractive when made of entire wheat bread between white slices.

### NILE SALAD

Cut cold boiled or roasted chicken in cubes (there should be one and one-half cups). Put

## Wedding Receptions

one-half cup English walnut meats in pan, sprinkle sparingly with salt, and add three-fourths tablespoon butter. Cook in a slow oven until browned and thoroughly heated, stirring occasionally; remove from oven, cool, break in pieces.

Mix chicken and nuts and marinate with French Dressing. Add three-fourths cup celery cut in small pieces. Arrange on a bed of lettuce, and mask with Mayonnaise Dressing.

### SALAD ROLLS

| | |
|---|---|
| 1 tablespoon sugar | ½ yeast cake |
| ¼ tablespoon salt | 2 tablespoons lukewarm |
| ½ cup scalded milk | water |
| 2 tablespoons melted butter | Flour |

Add sugar and salt to milk; when lukewarm, add yeast cake dissolved in lukewarm water and three-fourths cup flour. Cover and let rise until light, then add melted butter, and enough more flour to knead. Cover, again let rise, toss on a floured board, roll to one-half inch in thickness. Shape with a small round biscuit cutter dipped in flour, place in a buttered pan close together, let rise again, brush over with milk, and bake in a hot oven.

## Wedding Receptions

### MANHATTAN CREAM

| | |
|---|---|
| Yolks 5 eggs | 3 tablespoons brandy |
| 1 cup sugar | 1½ tablespoons vanilla |
| ½ teaspoon salt | Whites 5 eggs |
| 3 cups milk | 1½ cups heavy cream |

Make a custard of first four ingredients, strain, and cool. Add flavoring, whites of eggs beaten until stiff, and cream beaten until stiff. Freeze and mold in brick form. Serve with fresh strawberries cut in halves and sprinkled with sugar. If fresh fruit is not in season, substitute canned.

### POUND CAKES

| | |
|---|---|
| 1 cup butter (scant) | 5 eggs |
| 1½ cups flour | 1½ cups powdered sugar |
| 1 teaspoon vanilla | 1 teaspoon baking powder |

Cream the butter, and add flour gradually while beating constantly. Beat the yolks of the eggs until thick and lemon colored, and add sugar gradually. Combine mixtures, add whites of eggs, beaten until stiff, and sift over baking powder. Beat thoroughly, turn into a buttered shallow pan, and bake in a moderate oven.

Remove from pan, cut in one and one-half inch squares, circles, diamonds, or any fancy shapes. Cover with White Mountain Frosting and dec-

## Wedding Receptions

orate with nut meats, shredded cocoanut, candied cherries, violets, or rose leaves.

### WHITE MOUNTAIN FROSTING

1 cup sugar  
⅓ cup boiling water  
1 teaspoon vanilla or  
½ tablespoon lemon juice  
White 1 egg

Put sugar and water in saucepan and stir to prevent sugar from adhering to saucepan, heat gradually to boiling-point, and boil without stirring until syrup will thread when dropped from tip of spoon or tines of silver fork. Pour syrup gradually on beaten white of egg, beating mixture constantly, and continue beating until of right consistency to spread, then add flavoring and spread evenly with back of spoon.

### BRIDE'S CAKE

½ cup butter  
1½ cups sugar  
½ cup milk  
2½ cups flour  
3 teaspoons baking powder  
¼ teaspoon cream of tartar  
½ teaspoon almond extract  
Whites 6 eggs

Cream butter and sugar gradually while beating constantly; then add milk, flour mixed and sifted with baking powder, and cream of tartar and extract. Beat thoroughly and add whites

of eggs beaten until stiff. Bake in a buttered and floured round pan in a moderate oven. Cover with White Mountain Cream, decorate with ornamental frosting, arrange on a lace paper doiley, and surround with flowers to correspond with table decorations.

### GLACÈ FRUITS

2 cups sugar     1 cup boiling water
⅓ teaspoon cream of tartar

Put ingredients in a smooth saucepan, stir, place on range, and heat to boiling-point. Boil without stirring until syrup begins to discolor, which is 310° F. Wash off sugar which adheres to sides of saucepan, as in making fondant. Remove saucepan from fire, and place in a larger pan of cold water to instantly stop boiling. Remove from cold water and place in a saucepan of hot water during dipping. Dip grapes, strawberries, or sections of oranges or mandarins in syrup to cover, remove from syrup, and place on oiled paper.

BIRTHDAY FEASTING

# Birthday Feasting

## MENU No. I

*"As much valor is to be found in feasting as in fighting."*

Royal Canapés      Oysters on Half Shell

Celery      Brown Bread Sandwiches

Consommé Japonnaise      Bread Sticks

Fried Brook Trout      Sauce Tartare

Sliced Cucumbers      Roast Saddle of Venison

Currant Jelly Sauce

Broiled Kidneys      O'Brion Potatoes

French String Beans      Parisian Dressed Lettuce

Colonial Club Sandwiches      Frozen Pudding

Salted Almonds      Ginger Chips

Toasted Crackers      Roquefort

Café Noir

## ROYAL CANAPÉS

Fry one-half tablespoon finely chopped onion, three tablespoons butter, and one-third cup chopped mushroom caps five minutes. Add two tablespoons flour and stir until well blended; then pour on gradually while stirring constantly two-thirds cup cream. Bring to the boiling-point and add one cup finnan haddie (soaked in lukewarm water to cover forty-five minutes, then separated into flakes), two tablespoons grated cheese, and yolks two eggs slightly beaten. Season with salt and cayenne and pile on circular pieces of bread toasted on one side, having mixture on untoasted side. Sprinkle with grated cheese, then with buttered soft bread crumbs, and bake until crumbs are browned. Serve at once on small plates.

## CONSOMMÉ JAPONNAISE

| | |
|---|---|
| 2 lbs lean beef | 10 peppercorns |
| 3 lbs shin of beef | 3 cloves |
| Bones from roast chicken | 5 allspice berries |
| 1 carrot, sliced | 1 bay leaf |
| 1 onion, sliced | ¼ teaspoon thyme |
| 1 clove garlic | 1 quart cold water |
| 1 stalk celery, 1 sprig parsley, 1 leek, each cut in small pieces | 1½ quarts boiling water Salt Pepper |

## Birthday Feasting

Cut lean beef in small pieces and put in kettle with shin and chicken bones. Add vegetables, seasonings, and cold water, cover, and let stand one hour. Bring to the boiling-point and let boil, stirring constantly five minutes. Add boiling water and let simmer two and one-half hours. Season with salt and pepper, and strain through a fine strainer.

### BREAD STICKS

| | |
|---|---|
| 1 cup scalded milk | 1 yeast cake dissolved in |
| ¼ cup butter | ¼ cup lukewarm water |
| 1½ tablespoons sugar | White 1 egg |
| ½ teaspoon salt | 3¾ cups flour |

Add butter, sugar, and salt to milk; when lukewarm, add dissolved yeast cake, white of egg well beaten, and flour. Knead, let rise, shape, let rise again, and start baking in a hot oven, reducing heat that sticks may be crisp and dry. To shape sticks, first shape as small biscuits, roll on board (where there is no flour) with hands until eight inches in length, keeping of uniform size and rounded ends, which may be done by bringing fingers close to, but not over, ends of sticks.

## Birthday Feasting

### FRIED BROOK TROUT

Clean fish, leaving on heads and tails. Sprinkle with salt and pepper, dip in flour, egg, and crumbs, and fry three to four minutes in deep fat. As soon as trout are put into fat, remove fat to back of range so that they may not become too brown before cooked through. Arrange on hot platter and garnish with parsley and slices of lemon. Serve with Sauce Tartare.

### SAUCE TARTARE

½ teaspoon mustard  
1 teaspoon powdered sugar  
½ teaspoon salt  
Few grains cayenne  
Yolks 2 eggs  
½ cup olive oil  

1½ tablespoons vinegar  
Capers ⎫  
Pickles ⎬ ½ tablespoon,  
Olives ⎪ each, finely  
Parsley ⎭ chopped  

½ shallot, finely chopped  
¼ teaspoon powdered tarragon

Mix mustard, sugar, salt, and cayenne; add yolks of eggs, and stir until thoroughly mixed, setting bowl in pan of ice-water. Add oil, at first drop by drop, stirring with a wooden spoon or wire whisk. As mixture thickens, dilute with vinegar, when oil may be added more rapidly. Keep in cool place until ready to serve, then add remaining ingredients.

# Birthday Feasting

## ROAST SADDLE OF VENISON

Wipe meat, sprinkle with salt and pepper, place on rack in dripping pan, and dredge meat and bottom of pan with flour. Put in pan one slice onion, one slice carrot, and two stalks celery, cut in small pieces. Bake in hot oven fifty minutes, basting every ten minutes with one-third cup melted butter to which is added three tablespoons boiling water. Remove to hot platter and serve with

## CURRANT JELLY SAUCE

To three tablespoons fat remaining in pan add three tablespoons flour, and pour on, gradually, one cup chicken stock. Bring to boiling-point and add one-fourth cup Madeira wine and one-fourth cup currant jelly; strain, season with salt, and serve very hot.

## O'BRION POTATOES

Fry three cups potato cubes or balls in deep fat, drain on brown paper, and sprinkle with salt. Cook one slice onion in one and one-half tablespoons butter three minutes, remove onion, and add to butter three canned pimientos cut in small pieces. When thoroughly heated, add

potatoes; stir until well mixed, turn into serving dish, and sprinkle with finely chopped parsley.

## FRENCH STRING BEANS

Remove beans from can, put in a strainer, and pour over two quarts cold water. Drain and let stand exposed to the air one-half hour. Heat very hot and season with butter and salt.

## BROILED KIDNEYS

Order veal kidneys with the suet left on. Trim, split, and broil ten minutes. Arrange on pieces of toast and pour over melted butter seasoned with salt, cayenne, and lemon juice. Garnish with parsley.

## PARISIAN DRESSED LETTUCE

Wash lettuce, drain, and arrange in salad bowl. Just before serving pour over

## PARISIAN FRENCH DRESSING

½ teaspoon salt    4 tablespoons red wine
¼ teaspoon paprika    vinegar
    4 tablespoons olive oil

Mix ingredients and stir until well blended.

## COLONIAL CLUB SANDWICHES

Mash a cream cheese and moisten with cream until of right consistency to spread. Add one-fourth the quantity of finely chopped olives and season with salt and paprika.

Spread between slices of bread, remove crusts, and cut in fancy shapes.

## FROZEN PUDDING

2½ cups milk  1 cup heavy cream
1 cup sugar  ¼ cup rum
⅛ teaspoon salt  1 cup candied fruit, cherries,
2 eggs  pineapples, pears, and apri-
Brandy  cots

Cut fruit in small pieces, and soak two or three hours in brandy to cover, which prevents fruit from freezing. Make a custard of milk, sugar, salt, and eggs, strain, cool, add cream and rum, then freeze. Fill a brick mold with alternate layers of the cream and fruit; pack in salt and ice and let stand two hours.

## SALTED ALMONDS

See pages 5 and 6, under New Year's Afternoon Teas, Menu No. I.

# Birthday Feasting

## MENU NO. II

A BIRTHDAY LUNCHEON (FOR DÉBUTANTE DAUGHTER)

*"Standing with reluctant feet
Where the brook and river meet
Womanhood and childhood fleet."*
                                    Longfellow.

Bisque of Oysters

Olives        Celery        Salted Almonds

Halibut Cutlets        Luncheon Rolls

Lamb Chops à la Sabine

French Peas        Persillade Potatoes

Grapefruit Salad        Butter Thins

Bonbons

Pistachio Parfait        Marguerites

## Birthday Feasting

### BISQUE OF OYSTERS

Parboil one quart oysters in their own liquor, strain, reserve liquor, and finely chop the oysters. To the liquor add one and one-half quarts water, two stalks celery, two leeks, two slices onion, two sprigs parsley, two cloves, one-half bay leaf, the chopped oysters, one-half cup rice, and one pint milk. Let simmer one and one-fourth hours. Press through a sieve, add two teaspoons salt, one-eighth teaspoon each of nutmeg, cayenne, and pepper, and two egg yolks diluted with one cup cream. Serve in bouillon cups.

### SALTED ALMONDS

See pages 5 and 6, under New Year's Afternoon Teas, Menu No. I.

### HALIBUT CUTLETS

| | |
|---|---|
| ½ tablespoon shallot, finely chopped | 1 teaspoon salt |
| | ¼ teaspoon paprika |
| 2 tablespoons red pepper, finely chopped | ½ cup milk |
| | ½ cup cream |
| 3 tablespoons butter | 1¾ cups cold flaked cooked halibut |
| ⅓ cup flour | |

Cook shallot, pepper, and butter five minutes, stirring constantly. Add flour and seasonings and stir until well blended, then pour on gradu-

# Birthday Feasting

ally, while stirring constantly, milk and cream. Bring to the boiling-point and add flaked halibut. Cool, shape, dip in crumbs, egg and crumbs, fry in deep fat, and drain.

## LUNCHEON ROLLS

Add one tablespoon sugar and one-fourth teaspoon salt to one-half cup scalded milk; when lukewarm, add one-half yeast cake dissolved in two tablespoons lukewarm water and three-fourths cup flour. Cover and let rise, then add two tablespoons melted butter and flour to knead. Let rise again, roll to one-half inch thickness, shape with small round biscuit cutter, place in buttered pan, prick with a fork, let rise again, and bake. Brush over with melted butter and return to oven for one minute.

## LAMB CHOPS À LA SABINE

Gash six French chops by cutting through meat nearly to bone and stuff with the following: Mix six tablespoons soft bread crumbs, two and one-half tablespoons chopped cooked ham, two and one-half tablespoons chopped mushroom caps, two tablespoons melted butter, and salt and cayenne to taste. Dip in crumbs, egg and crumbs,

and fry in deep fat four minutes. Remove to hot serving dish and pour around

## MADEIRA SAUCE

Melt three tablespoons butter, add three tablespoons flour, and stir until well blended, then pour on gradually, while stirring constantly, one cup milk and one-half cup heavy cream. Bring to the boiling-point and add two chopped truffles, two tablespoons Madeira wine, and salt and pepper to taste. If truffles are not at hand, omit them.

## PERSILLADE POTATOES

To five riced potatoes add three tablespoons butter, one teaspoon salt, a few grains pepper, and one-third cup hot milk. Beat with a fork until creamy and pile on a dish. Beat one-half cup heavy cream until stiff, add one-half cup grated mild cheese and season with salt and pepper. Spread over the potatoes and set in a very hot oven to melt cheese and brown cream.

## GRAPEFRUIT SALAD

Drain canned artichoke bottoms, marinate with French Dressing, cover, and let stand in a cold place until thoroughly chilled. Mound with grapefruit pulp, which has also been drained and

# Birthday Feasting

marinated, arrange in nests of lettuce leaves, pour over French Dressing, and garnish with strips of red pepper.

## PISTACHIO PARFAIT

| | |
|---|---|
| 1 cup sugar | 1 teaspoon almond extract |
| ¼ cup water | 1 pint thick cream |
| Whites 3 eggs | Leaf green |
| 1 tablespoon vanilla | ½ cup chopped pistachio nuts |

Cook sugar and water until syrup will thread when dropped from tip of spoon. Pour slowly, while beating constantly, on to whites of eggs beaten until stiff, and continue the beating until mixture is cold. Color cream a delicate green and beat until stiff. Combine mixtures, add flavorings and nut meats, and freeze, using three parts finely crushed ice to one part rock salt. Mold in brick form and pack in salt and ice. Remove from mold and surround with whipped cream, sweetened and flavored with vanilla. Sprinkle with chopped pistachio nuts.

## MARGUERITES

| | |
|---|---|
| 2 eggs | ¼ teaspoon baking powder |
| 1 cup brown sugar | ⅓ teaspoon salt |
| ½ cup flour | 1 cup pecan nut meats, cut in small pieces |

Beat eggs slightly, and add remaining ingredients in the order given. Fill small buttered tins (tins much smaller than muffin pans) two-thirds full of mixture, and place pecan nut meat on each. Bake in a moderate oven fifteen minutes.

CHILDREN'S BIRTHDAY PARTIES

## Children's Birthday Parties

### MENU NO. I.

*"Let them exult, their laugh and song
Are rarely known to last too long,
Let us not strive
To knock their fairy castles down."*

Boylston Sandwiches        Lenox Sandwiches

Neapolitan Ice Cream

Angel Birthday Cake

Small Hard Candies in Favor Boxes

Raspberry Shrub

220   Children's Birthday Parties

### BOYLSTON SANDWICHES

Mash a cream cheese, add two and one-half tablespoons peanut butter, and work until well blended, then season with salt. Spread between thin slices of Graham bread, put together in pairs, remove crusts, and cut into fancy shapes. Arrange on a plate covered with a doiley.

### LENOX SANDWICHES

Work one-fourth cup almond paste until smooth. Add one-fourth cup powdered sugar and a few grains salt. When well blended, moisten with three-eighths cup heavy cream. Spread thin slices of buttered white bread with mixture, cover with buttered bread, remove crusts, and cut in any desired shapes—triangles, squares, finger-shaped pieces, hearts, diamonds, etc. Arrange on a plate covered with a doiley.

Almond paste may be bought in one-pound tins of any first-class city grocer.

### NEAPOLITAN ICE CREAM

Pack orange ice cream and chocolate ice cream in layers of equal depth in a brick mold. Pack in salt and ice (using four parts finely crushed ice to one part rock salt) and let stand two hours.

# Children's Birthday Parties

Remove from mold to chilled dish and cut in slices for serving.

## ORANGE ICE

4 cups water  
2 cups sugar  
¼ cup lemon juice  
Grated rind of two oranges  
2 cups orange juice

Mix ingredients, cover, and let stand one hour. Strain and freeze, using three parts finely crushed ice to one part rock salt.

## MACAROON ICE CREAM

1 quart cream  
1 cup macaroons  
¾ cup sugar  
1 tablespoon vanilla

Dry, pound, and measure macaroons; add to cream, then add sugar and vanilla. Freeze, using three parts finely crushed ice to one part rock salt.

## CHOCOLATE ICE CREAM

1 quart thin cream  
1 cup sugar  
Few grains salt  
1½ squares Baker's chocolate  
Hot water  
1 tablespoon vanilla

Melt chocolate and dilute with hot water to pour easily, add to cream; then add sugar, salt, and flavoring, and freeze.

## ANGEL CAKE

Whites 5 eggs ½ teaspoon cream of tartar
¾ cup sugar ½ cup bread flour
1 teaspoon vanilla

Beat whites of eggs until stiff and dry and add gradually, while beating constantly, sugar (fine granulated) mixed and sifted with cream of tartar. Sift flour into mixture, add vanilla, and cut and fold until blended. Turn into a buttered and floured angel-cake pan and bake in a moderate oven. Remove from pan, cover with White Mountain Frosting, and ornament with small candles placed in flower cases. The little cases may be bought of first-class city grocers or dealers in confectioners' supplies.

## WHITE MOUNTAIN FROSTING

1 cup sugar 1 teaspoon vanilla or
⅓ cup boiling water ½ tablespoon lemon juice
Whites 2 eggs

Put sugar and water in saucepan, and stir to prevent sugar from adhering to saucepan; heat gradually to boiling-point, and boil without stirring until syrup will thread when dropped from tip of spoon or tines of silver fork. Pour syrup gradually on beaten white of egg, beating

# Children's Birthday Parties

mixture constantly, and continue beating until of right consistency to spread; then add flavoring and pour over cake, spreading evenly with back of spoon. Crease as soon as firm. If not beaten long enough, frosting will run; if beaten too long, it will not be smooth. Frosting beaten too long may be improved by adding a few drops of lemon juice or boiling water. This frosting is soft inside and has a glossy surface.

## RASPBERRY SHRUB

3 quarts raspberries    1 pint cider vinegar
Cut sugar

Pick over raspberries, put one-half in earthen jar, add vinegar, cover, and let stand twenty-four hours. Strain through double thickness cheese-cloth. Pour liquor over remaining raspberries and let stand twenty-four hours.

Again strain liquor through double thickness cheese-cloth. To each cup juice add one-half pound sugar. Heat gradually until sugar is dissolved, then let boil twenty minutes. Bottle and cork. Dilute with water for serving.

## Children's Birthday Parties

### MENU NO. II.

*"Show me your nest with your young ones in it;
I will not steal them away,
I am old! You may trust me, linnet, linnet,
I am seven times one to-day."*

      Jean Ingelow.

Honey Sandwiches   Chicken Cream Sandwiches

Strawberry Ice   and   Vanilla Ice Cream

Cocoanut Kisses

Sunshine Birthday Cake

Sweet Chocolate

Cap Bonbons

## 226  Children's Birthday Parties

### HONEY SANDWICHES

Spread thin slices of buttered white bread with Quince Honey. Put together in pairs, remove crusts, cut in fancy shapes, and arrange on a plate covered with a lace paper doiley.

### QUINCE HONEY

5 large quinces          5 lbs. sugar
2 cups boiling water

Pare and grate quinces. Add sugar to water and stir over range until sugar is dissolved; then add quinces. Let simmer fifteen minutes and turn into jelly glasses. Cover when cold.

### CHICKEN CREAM SANDWICHES

Finely chop three-fourths cup breast meat from a cooked fowl, add one-fourth cup finely cut celery, and one cup rich milk. Heat to boiling-point and add a boiled mashed onion and three tablespoons flour mixed with two tablespoons butter. Cook until thick, then add whites two eggs beaten until stiff, salt, pepper, and lemon juice to taste. Turn into mold, first dipped in cold water, and let stand twelve hours. Remove from mold and spread between thin slices buttered bread. Remove crusts and cut in fancy shapes.

## STRAWBERRY ICE AND VANILLA ICE CREAM

Pack strawberry ice and vanilla ice cream in brick mold. Pack in salt and ice and let stand two hours. Remove from mold to chilled dish and cut in slices for serving.

### STRAWBERRY ICE

| | |
|---|---|
| 4 cups water | 2 cups strawberry juice |
| 1½ cups sugar | 1 tablespoon lemon juice |

Make a syrup by boiling water and sugar twenty minutes. Add strawberries, mashed and squeezed through a double thickness of cheesecloth, then add lemon juice, strain, and freeze.

### VANILLA ICE CREAM

| | |
|---|---|
| 2 cups scalded milk | 1 egg |
| 1 tablespoon flour | ⅛ teaspoon salt |
| 1 cup sugar | 1 quart thin cream |
| 2 tablespoons vanilla | |

Mix flour, sugar, and salt, add egg slightly beaten, and milk gradually; cook over hot water twenty minutes, stirring constantly at first; should custard have curdled appearance, it will disappear in freezing. When cool, add cream and flavoring, strain and freeze.

## COCOANUT KISSES

Whites 2 eggs  
½ cup fine granulated sugar  
¼ teaspoon vanilla  
3 tablespoons shredded cocoanut

Beat the whites of eggs until stiff and add gradually, while beating constantly, the sugar, continue the beating until mixture will hold its shape. Cut and fold in remaining sugar and add flavoring and cocoanut.

Shape with a tablespoon or pastry bag and tube on wet board covered with letter paper. Bake thirty minutes in a moderate oven.

## SUNSHINE BIRTHDAY CAKE

Whites 5 eggs  
¼ teaspoon salt  
½ teaspoon cream of tartar  
Yolks 3 eggs  
¾ cup sugar  
½ teaspoon almond extract  
½ cup pastry flour

Add salt to whites of eggs and beat until light. Sift in cream of tartar and beat until stiff. Beat yolks of eggs until thick and lemon colored and add two heaping tablespoons beaten whites. To remaining whites add gradually sugar measured after five siftings. Add almond extract and combine mixtures. Cut and fold in flour

## Children's Birthday Parties

measured after five siftings. Bake in angel-cake pan, first dipped in cold water, in a slow oven one hour. Have a pan of hot water in oven during the baking.

Remove from pan, frost and decorate, same as Angel Birthday Cake.

# INDEX

ALMOND Cream, 57
Almonds, Salted, 5
Anchovied Potatoes in Shells, 92
Angel Birthday Cake, 222
Apple Baskets, 170
Apricot Bombe, 64
Armour, Parfait, 174
Asparagus, Ambassadrice Capon with, 91
Attleboro Sandwiches, 4

BALTIMORE Cake, Lady 111
    Lord, 35
Batonet Potatoes, 74
Beans, French String, 208
Beef, Tournadoes of, 74
Bement à la, Sweet Potatoes, 148
Birthday Cake, Angel, 222
    Sunshine, 228
Biscuit, Macaroon Strawberry, 110
Bisque of Oysters, 211
    Pimiento, 98
Bouillon, Iced Tomato, 108
    Manhattan Clam, 44
Boylston Sandwiches, 220
Brandy and Hot Sauce, 182
    Sauce, Foamy, 154

Bread and Butter Folds, 196
    Brown, 131
    Entire Wheat, 102
    Pulled, 168
    Sandwiches, Brown, 130
        Entire Wheat, 103
    Sticks, 205
Breslin Patties, 180
Brides Cake, 199
Britannia, Perch, 90
Brook Trout, Fried, 206
Brown Bread, 131
    Sandwiches, 130
    Gravy, 148
    Soup Stock, 178
Butter Folds, Bread and, 196
    Pimiento, 33
Buttered Educator Crackers, 8

CADILLAC Cheese Sandwiches, 39
Cake, Angel Birthday, 222
    Bride's, 199
    Lady Baltimore, 111
    Lord Baltimore, 35
    Quality, 65
    Raised Fruit Loaf, 131
    Sunshine Birthday, 228
    Wedding, 191

# Index

Cakes, Cheese, 76
  Pound, 198
  Silver Sponge, 24
Canapes, Dexter, 85
  Rectors, 98
  Royal, 204
  Shamrock, 80
  Thorndike, 44
Candied Orange Peel, 63
Capon with Asparagus, Ambassadrice, 91
Caramel Coffee Parfait, 33
Carrots with Peas, Glazed, 100
Cases, Timbale, 30
Cauliflower, Hongroise, 171
Caviare, Celery with, 158
Celery with Caviare, 158
  Roquefort Cheese, 179
Chantilly Mousse, 94
Chaudfroid of Salmon, 55
Cheese Cakes, 76
  Celery with Roquefort, 179
  Sandwiches, Cadillac, 39
  Stars, 172
Cherry Salad, 62
Chestnut Gravy, 159
Chicken Consommé with Oysters, 168
  Cream Sandwiches, 226
  Forcemeat, 122
  Huntington, 21
  Jelly Salad, 38
  King, à la, 188
· Knickerbocker, Suprême of, 46
  Pie, 152
  Timbales, Traymore, 54

Chiffonade Dressed Lettuce, 153
  Dressing, 153
Chocolate with Whipped Cream, Hot, 11
  Ice Cream, 221
  Marshmallow Sauce, 48
Chops à la Sabine, Lamb, 212
Christmas Salad, 172
Cinkities, 40
Clam Bouillon, Manhattan, 44
Claret Punch, 120
Club Sandwiches, Colonial, 209
Cocktail, Oyster, 72
  Sardine, 168
Cocoa, Five O'clock, 17
Cocoanut Kisses, 228
  Rings, 111
Coffee, 132
  Caramel Parfait, 33
Cole Slaw, 82
Colonial Club Sandwiches, 209
Condes, 85
Confectioners' Frosting, 40
Conserve, Cranberry, 149
  Peach, 4
Consommé, 177
  Filippini, 176
  Japonnaise, 204
  with Oysters, Chicken. 168
Cookies, Nut Ginger, 141
  Scotch Five O'clock Tea, 9

# Index

Cork Timbales, 75
Corn, Priscilla Popped, 130, 132
Coupe Moquin, 183
Crab Meat Mornay, 92
Crackers, Buttered Educator, 8
  Crisp, 73
  Souffled, 98
Cranberries, Frozen, 161
Cranberry Conserve, 149
Cream, Almond, 57
  Dressing, 82
  French Dressing, 161
  Macaroon, 110
  Manhattan, 198
  Pimiento, 45
  Potatoes in, 180
  Sandwiches, Chicken, 226
  Sauce, 101
  Whipped, Hot Chocolate with, 11
Crisp Crackers, 73
Crisps, Peanut, 14
Croquettes, Potato and Spinach, 160
  St Denis, 180
  Shapleigh, 62
  Turnip, 149
Crushed Strawberries, Orange Ice Cream with, 118
Cucumber Cups, 161
  Ribbons, 99
  Sauce, 56
Cups, Cucumber, 161
Currant Jelly Sauce, 207
  Mint Sauce, 100
Cutlets, Halibut, 211

Dates, Stuffed, 164
Delight, Turkish, 16
Delmonico Dressing, 172
Devonshire Sandwiches, 8
Dewey Sauce, 163
Dexter Canapes, 90
Dressed Lettuce, Chiffonade, 153
  Parisian, 208
Dressing, Chiffonade, 153
  Cream, 82
  French, 161
  Delmonico, 172
  Mayonnaise, 94
  Parisian French, 208
Duck, Roast, 179

Easter Salad, 93
Educator Crackers, Buttered, 8
Entire Wheat Bread, 102
  Sandwiches, 103
Epicurean Sauce, 32

Fairmont Sandwiches, 56
Figs, Knickerbocker, 66
Filippini Consommé, 176
Fillets of Halibut à la Hollenden, 45
  Loomis, 81
Filling, Fruit and Nut, 112
  Lobster, 20
  Orange, 16
Finger Rolls, 117
  Sticks, 91
Fingers, Lady, 41
Five O'clock Cocoa, 17
  Tea, 6
  Teas, Scotch, 9
Florida Orange Sticks, 15

## Index

Foamy Brandy Sauce, 154
Folds, Bread and Butter, 196
Forcemeat, Chicken, 122
Fourth of July Punch, 113
French Dressing, Cream, 161
  Parisian, 208
  String Beans, 208
  Vanilla Ice Cream, 163
Frosting, Confectioners', 40
  Ice Cream, 35, 112
  Orange, 34
  Ornamental, 192
  Portsmouth, 132
  Quality, 66
  White Mountain, 199, 222
Frozen Cranberries, 161
  Pudding, 209
Fruit with Apricot Brandy, Grape, 176
  Loaf, Raised, 131
  and Nut Filling, 112
  Pudding, 173
  Punch, 59, 125
  Salad, Grape, 213
Fruits, Glacè, 200
Fudge, Sultana, 136

GANSER Salad, 130
George Washington Hatchets, 58
German Punch, 137
Giblet Stuffing, 159
Ginger Cookies, Nut, 141
Glacè Fruits, 200
Glazed Carrots with Peas, 100
  Silver Skin Onions, 160

Goose with Potato Stuffing, Roast, 170
Graham Sandwiches, 124
Grape Fruit Salad, 213
  with Apricot Brandy, 176
Gravy, Brown, 148
  Chestnut, 159

HADDON Hall Halibut, 73
Halibut au Lit, 99
  Cutlets, 211
  Fillets, 45
  of Loomis, 81
  Haddon Hall, 73
  à la Hallenden, Fillets of, 45
  Tyrolienne, 123
Hamlin Ham Timbales, 140
Ham Mousse, 32
  Timbales, Hamlin, 140
Harvard Wafers, 49
Hearts, Orange, 33
Hickory Nougat, 10
Hollenden, à la, Fillets of Halibut, 45
Honey Sandwiches, Orange, 22
  Quince, 226
Hongroise, Cauliflower, 171
Honor Sandwiches, 32
Horseradish Sauce, Jellied Veal, 117
Hot Sauce, Brandy and, 182
Huntington Chicken, 21
  à la Sweetbreads, 101

ICE, Orange, 221
  Strawberry, 191, 227
Iceberg, Irish, 76

# Index

Ice Cream, Chocolate, 48, 221
  with Marshmallow Sauce, 48
  French Vanilla, 163
  Frosting, 35, 112
  Macaroon, 221
  Neapolitan, 220
  Orange, with Crushed Strawberries, 118
  Pistachio, with Peach Sauce, 84
  Praline, 64
  Strawberry, 124
  Vanilla, 227
Iced Tea, 17
  Tomato Bouillon, 108
Imperial Sticks, 81
Irish Iceberg, 76

JAFFA Spanish Mackerel, 169
Jam Jumbles, 4
Japonnaise Consommé, 204
Jellied Veal, Horseradish Sauce, 117
Jelly, Orange, 101
  Rolls, Pastry, 164
  Salad, Chicken, 38
  Sauce, Currant, 207
  Wine, 57
July Punch, Fourth of, 113
Jumbles, Jam, 4

KERNELS of Pork, 83
Kidneys, Broiled, 208
Kisses, Cocoanut, 228
Knickerbocker Figs, 66
  Suprême of Chicken, 46

LADY Baltimore Cake, 111
  Fingers, 41
Lakewood Salad, 47
Lamb Chops à la Sabine, 212
  Roast Crown of, 100
Layer Sandwiches, 62
Lemon Queens, 119
Lenox Sandwiches, 109, 220
Lettuce, Chiffonade Dressed, 153
  Parisian, 208
  Sandwiches, 188
Loaf, Quick Nut, 14
  Raised Fruit, 131
Lobster Filling, 20
  Lucullus, 116
  Patties, 20
Loomis, Fillets of Halibut, 81
  Sauce, 82
Lord Baltimore Cake, 35
Lucullus Lobster, 116
Luncheon Rolls, 46, 212

MACAROON Cream, 110
  Ice Cream, 221
Macaroons, 24
  Mock, 104
  Strawberry Biscuit, 110
Mackerel, Jaffa Spanish, 169
Madeira Sauce, 213
Malaga Salad, 84, 102
Manhattan Clam Bouillon, 44
  Cream, 198
Marguerites, 214
Marmalade, Orange, 8, 34
Marshmallow Sauce, Chocolate Ice Cream with, 48

# 236    Index

Martinique Potatoes, 47
Mayonnaise Dressing, 94
  Piquante, 93
  Salmon, 188
Meat, Mince Pie, 155
Meringues, 95
Meringue Squares, Walnut, 5
Mince Pie, 156
  Meat, 155
Mint Paste, 104
  Sauce Currant, 100
  Tulip, 36
Mock Macaroons, 104
Molded Sweetbreads, Truffle Sauce, 122
Monroe Sauce, 173
Moquin, Coupe, 183
Mornay, Crab Meat, 92
Mousse, Chantilly, 94
  Ham, 32
  Pineapple, 23
Mousselaine Sauce, 162
Mushroom Sauce, 99
  Soup, 87

Neapolitan Ice Cream, 220
Neuremburghs, 125
New England Thanksgiving Pudding, 162
Nile Salad, 196
Noisette Sandwiches, 14
Nougat, Hickory, 10
Nut Ginger Cookies, 141
  Loaf, Quick, 141
  Wafers, 119

Oat Wafers, 65
O'Brien Potatoes, 207

Onions, Boiled, 148
  Glazed Silver Skin, 160
  Stuffed, 83
Orange Filling, 16
  Frosting, 34
  Hearts, 33
  Honey, 23
  Sandwiches, 22
Ice, 221
  Cream with Crushed Strawberries, 118
  Jelly, 103
  Marmalade, 8, 34
  Peel, Candied, 63
  Sticks, Florida, 15
Oriental Punch, 25
Ornamental Frosting, 192
Oyster Cocktail, 72
  Soup, 158
Oysters, Bisque of, 211
  Chicken Consommé with, 168
  with Sherry, 146

Parfait Armour 174
  Caramel Coffee, 33
  Pistachio, 214
Parisian Dressed Lettuce, 208
  French Dressing, 208
Paste, Mint, 104
Puff, 149
Quality, 154
Pastry Jelly Rolls, 164
Patties, Breslin, 180
  Lobster, 20
Patty Shells, 20
Peach Conserve, 4
  Sauce, Pistachio Ice Cream with, 84

# Index

Peanut Crisps, 14
  Drops, 58
Peas, Glazed Carrots with, 100
Pecans, Salted, 169
Peel, Candied Orange, 63
Peneuche, 141
Perch Britannia, 90
Persillade Potatoes, 213
Pie, Chicken, 152
  Mince, 156
  Pumpkin, 156
Pimiento Bisque, 98
  Butter, 33
  Cream, 45
Pineapple Mousse, 23
  Punch, 193
  Sponge, 39
Piquante, Mayonnaise, 93
Pistachio Ice Cream with Peach Sauce, 84
  Parfait, 214
Plum Pudding, English, 182
Popped Corn, Priscilla, 132
Pork, Kernels of, 83
Portsmouth Frosting, 132
Potato Stuffing, Roast Goose with, 170
Potatoes à la Bement, Sweet, 148
  and Spinach Croquettes, 160
  Batonet, 74
  in Cream, 180
  in Shells, Anchovied, 90
  Martinique, 47
  O'Brion, 207
  Persillade, 213
  Rissolées, 101
  Savory, 83

Potatoes with Sherry, Sweet, 171
Pound Cakes, 198
Praline Ice Cream, 64
Priscilla Popped Corn, 132
Pudding, English Plum, 182
  Frozen, 209
  Fruit, 173
  New England Thanksgiving, 162
  Puritan, 153
  Wordsworth, 103
Puff Paste, 149
Pulled Bread, 168
Pumpkin Pie, 156
Punch, Claret, 120
  Fourth of July, 113
  Fruit, 59, 125
  German, 137
  Oriental, 25
  Pineapple, 193
  Puritan Pudding, 153

QUALITY Cake, 65
  Frosting, 66
  Paste, 154
Queens, Lemon, 119
Quick Nut Loaf, 14
Quince Honey, 226

RAISED Fruit Loaf, 131
Rarebit, Rob's, 136
Raspberry Shrub, 223
Rector's Canapes, 98
Ribbon Sandwiches, 140
Ribbons, Cucumber, 99
Rings, Cocoanut, 111
  Swedish, 124
Rissolées, Potatoes, 101
Roast Crown of Lamb, 100

## Index

Roast Duck, 179
  Goose, Potato Stuffing, 170
  Saddle of Venison, 207
  Stuffed Turkey, 146
Rob's Karebit, 136
Rochester Sandwiches, 15
Rolled Wafers, 77
Rolls, Finger, 117
  Luncheon, 46, 212
  Pastry Jelly, 164
  Reception, 189
  Salad, 55, 197
  Tea, 22
Roquefort Cheese, Celery with, 179
Royal Canapes, 204
Russian Tea, 10

SADDLE of Venison, Roast, 207
St Denis Croquettes, 180
St. Patrick Soup, 72
Salad, Cherry, 62
  Chicken Jelly, 38
  Christmas, 172
  Easter, 93
  Ganser, 130
  Grape Fruit, 213
  Lakewood, 47
  Malaga, 84, 102
  Nile, 196
  Rolls, 55, 197
  Shamrock, 75
  Stuffed Tomato, 181
  Sweetbread, 109
Salmon Balls, 108
  Chaudfroid of, 55
  Mayonnaise, 188
Salted Almonds, 5

Salted Pecans, 169
Sandwiches, Attleboro, 4
  Boylston, 220
  Brown Bread, 130
  Cadillac Cheese, 39
  Chicken Cream, 226
  Colonial Club, 209
  Devonshire, 8
  Entire Wheat Bread, 103
  Fairmont, 56
  Graham, 124
  Honey, 226
  Honor, 32
  Layer, 62
  Lenox, 109, 220
  Lettuce, 188
  Noisette, 14
  Orange Honey, 22
  Ribbon, 140
  Rochester, 15
  Sembrich, 118
  Somerset, 181
Sardine Cocktail, 168
Sauce, Brandy and Hot, 182
  Cream, 101
  Cucumber, 56
  Currant Jelly, 207
  Mint, 100
  Dewey, 163
  Epicurean, 32
  Foamy Brandy, 154
  Horseradish, Jellied Veal, 117
  Hot, Brandy and, 182
  Loomis, 82
  Madeira, 213
  Marshmallow, Chocolate Ice Cream with, 48
  Monroe, 173
  Mousselaine, 162

# Index

Sauce, Mushroom, 73, 99
  Peach, Pistachio Ice Cream with, 84
  Tartare, 206
  Truffle, Molded Sweetbreads, 122
  Tyrolienne, 123
Savory Potatoes, 83
Scallops, Scalloped, 38
Sedalia Sticks, 63
Sembrich Sandwiches, 118
Shamrock Canapes, 80
  Salad, 75
Shapleigh Croquettes, 62
Shells, Patty, 20
Shrimps a la Newburg, 196
Shrub, Raspberry, 223
Silver Skin Onions, Glazed, 160
  Sponge Cakes, 24
Slaw, Cole, 82
Somerset Sandwiches, 181
Soubrics of Spinach, 74
Souffle, Squash, 160
Souffled Crackers, 98
Soup Stock, Brown, 178
  Mushroom, 85
  Oyster, 158
  St. Patrick, 72
  Spinach, 80
  Thanksgiving, 146
Spanish Mackerel, Jaffa, 169
Spinach Croquettes, Potato and, 160
  Soubrics of, 74
  Soup, 80
Sponge Cakes, Silver, 24
  Pineapple, 39
Squash Souffle, 160

Sticks, Bread, 205
  Finger, 91
  Florida Orange, 15
  Imperial, 81
  Sedalia, 63
  Sultana, 9
Stock, Brown Soup, 178
Strawberry Biscuit Macaroons, 110
  Bombe, 190
  Ice, 191, 227
  Cream, 124
String Beans, French, 208
Stuffed Dates, 164
  Onions, 83
  Roast Turkey, 147
  Tomato Salad, 181
Stuffing, 146
  Giblet, 159
  Potato, Roast Goose with, 170
Sultana Fudge, 136
  Sticks, 9
Sunshine Birthday Cake, 228
Suprême of Chicken, Knickerbocker, 46
Swedish Rings, 124
Sweetbread Salad, 109
Sweetbreads à la Huntington, 91
  York, 30
  Molded, Truffle Sauce, 122
Sweet Potatoes à la Bement, 148
  with Sherry, 171

Tartare, Sauce, 206
Tea, Five O'clock, 6

## Index

Tea, Iced, 17
   Rolls, 22
   Russian, 10
Teas, Scotch Five O'clock, 9
Thanksgiving Pudding, New England, 162
   Soup, 146
Thorndike Canapes, 44
Timbale Cases, 30
Timbales, Cork, 75
   Hamlin Ham, 140
   Traymore Chicken, 54
Tomato Bouillon, Iced, 108
   Salad, Stuffed, 181
Tournadoes of Beef, 74
Traymore Chicken Timbales, 54
Trout, Fried Brook, 206
Truffle Sauce, Molded Sweetbreads, 122
Tulip, Mint, 36
Turkey, Roast Stuffed, 147
Turkish Delight, 16
Turnip Croquettes, 149

Tyrolienne Halibut, 123
   Sauce, 123

VANILLA Ice Cream, 227
   French, 163
Veal, Jellied, Horseradish Sauce, 116, 117
Venison, Roast Saddle of, 207

WAFERS, Harvard, 49
   Nut, 119
   Oat, 65
   Rolled, 77
Walnut Meringue Squares 5
Washington Hatchets, George, 58
Wedding Cake, 191
Wheat Bread, Entire, 102
   Sandwiches, 103
White Mountain Frosting, 199
Wine Jelly, 57
Wordsworth Pudding, 101

www.ingramcontent.com/pod-product-compliance
Lightning Source LLC
Chambersburg PA
CBHW032105090426
42743CB00007B/247